Almon Gunnison

**Rambles Overland**

A Trip across the Continent

Almon Gunnison

**Rambles Overland**
*A Trip across the Continent*

ISBN/EAN: 9783337148188

Printed in Europe, USA, Canada, Australia, Japan

Cover: Foto ©Andreas Hilbeck / pixelio.de

More available books at **www.hansebooks.com**

# RAMBLES OVERLAND.

## A TRIP ACROSS THE CONTINENT.

ALMON GUNNISON.

WHAT THY SOUL HOLDS DEAR, IMAGINE IT
TO LIE THAT WAY THOU GO'ST.
       SHAKSPEARE.

BOSTON:
UNIVERSALIST PUBLISHING HOUSE.
1884.

*Copyright, 1883,*
BY UNIVERSALIST PUBLISHING HOUSE.

University Press:
JOHN WILSON AND SON, CAMBRIDGE.

# *PREFACE.*

*And so I penned
It down, until at last it came to be,
For length and breadth, the bigness which you see.*

BUNYAN.

# CONTENTS.

### CHAPTER I.
WESTWARD HO! . . . . . . . . . . . . . . 11

### CHAPTER II.
THE YELLOWSTONE PARK . . . . . . . . . 29

### CHAPTER III.
SAUNTERINGS IN WONDER-LAND . . . . . . . . 47

### CHAPTER IV.
A FIFTY-MILE WALK . . . . . . 65

### CHAPTER V.
OVER THE ROCKIES BY STAGE . . . . . 85

### CHAPTER VI.
ON THE PACIFIC SLOPE . . . . . 99

## CHAPTER VII.
|  | PAGE |
|---|---|
| THE CITY OF THE GOLDEN GATE | 109 |

## CHAPTER VIII.
THE APPROACH TO THE YOSEMITE . . . . . . . . 127

## CHAPTER IX.
THE YOSEMITE . . . . . . . . . . . . . 139

## CHAPTER X.
THE ORANGE-LAND OF CALIFORNIA . . . . . . . 159

## CHAPTER XI.
ACROSS THE DESERT . . . . . . . . . . . 181

## CHAPTER XII.
A MEXICAN DÉTOUR . . . . . . . . . . . 191

## CHAPTER XIII.
COLORADO DAYS . . . . . . . . . . . . 211

## CHAPTER XIV.
INCIDENTS OF TRAVEL . . . . . . . . . . 229

# WESTWARD HO!

*Go West, young man!*
HORACE GREELEY.

# RAMBLES OVERLAND.

## CHAPTER I.

### WESTWARD HO!

WHEN Madame de Sévigné rapturously exclaimed, "a journey to make, and Paris at the end of it!" she must have had the same emotions with which at midnight we commence our trip across the continent to the Golden Gate.

The Great Northern Railway approaches completion, and over the unfinished gap we shall make passage of the Rockies in a stage. The pictures of Moran have made us impatient to see the wonders of the Yellowstone; thence we will go southward on the Pacific, enter the Golden Gate, and come homeward by the Southern desert, with sight of orange groves and Mexico upon the way.

Our little party consists of four. A Dramatic Critic of the city press, with a clever knack at sketching and a kind of universal knowledge, picked up in his Bohemian wanderings up and down the earth; "the Reporter," not long from college, sent out with the benedictions of his paper, "to write the country up,"— a youth of most susceptible proclivities, and withal a kind of pushing enterprise that might by a less fastidious historian be accounted "cheek." A geological Professor and the writer complete the group. The Professor is a man not over old in years, nor always so sedate in manner as the world outside our camping-tent surmises, but skilled in lore of rocks and flowers, a much-travelled man, and, despite his business, not yet petrified into a "fossil," although the irreverent youngsters of the party early christen him "Old Silurian." At Washington we rendezvous. We push onward by the "Scenic Route," as it is advertised upon the bills; riding upon the platform in the exhilaration of our new-found freedom, taking note of the fair landscapes that lie along the roadway to the mountains, the canal-boat moving slowly on near the track, the captain sitting in the sun astride the tiller, while his wife beside the mule tugs on ahead.

At Harper's Ferry the iron horse makes pause to drink, and we see the engine-house held in the antebellum days by old John Brown. It has no historic look, for it is used as the showman's bulletin, and bears upon its front the portrait of the tattooed man, who is numbered among the wonders of "the greatest show on earth."

We have good fortune in the time of our passage through the heart of the Alleghanies, for the sun is four hours high when, at the mountain's base, the other engine is hitched on, and the great lumbering train slowly begins the long ascent. We have sent a telegram ahead to the division superintendent for leave to ride upon the engine, and so we make the passage in the engine's cab, half-blinded with the smoke and suffocated with the simmering oil. The view from our lofty perch is a royal one as the train moves up: great sweeps of valleys, sunlit peaks above, villages in cosiest nooks below, and ragged cliffs beside the track. The great engines pull heavily with panting breath, the engineer holding hand upon the lever, his long beard tied together with a cotton string; so with wonder all alert we come skyward to the summit, and with exultant speed go down into the valley. Just when the sunset of the second day is touching the waters of the lake we reach Chicago. How wonderful it is! What powers of expansion, what recuperative force, what magic has changed the prairie to a city, what bustle in the life of its crowded streets! There are young faces everywhere in places of authority; in bank and office, store and court, young men are in charge, and the world goes on despite their youth. Hotels, churches, public buildings, and business places give evidence of wealth, and though there is a little touch of the ostentation that suddenly acquired wealth affects, yet there is such tremendous energy of life in this bumptious city of the lake, that the casual visitor is not surprised that all the natives feel kinship with the Apostle Paul, in that, with him, they are "citizens of no mean city." The traces of the fire are nearly gone, and so out of ashes has beauty come, that, imitating Rome, which gave honored place to the image of the wolf that suckled the founders of the city, we would suggest — if it be permitted for the greater city to imitate the lesser one — that Mrs. O'Leary's cow be made Chicago's tutelary deity, held in honor for her works' sake, the worship finding precedent in the honors paid in Bible times to a certain golden calf.

On to the Northwest, crossing the Mississippi into the rival cities of St. Paul and Minneapolis, we hasten. Fourteen years ago we came hither from far below upon one of the palace steamers of the river. We do not find the levee now where it run itself aground for anchorage, nor is the little ferry across the stream, nor is the long ride by Fort Snelling and the Falls of Minnehaha as solitary as it used to be.

The cities have grown mightily, with streets of metropolitan dimensions, stores, houses, institutions, everything that great cities in the older States acquire in centuries. Unless the outlook is deceptive, here is to be the emporium of the great Northwest.

The cities will grow together and become the distributing centre for this vast empire lying between the lake and the seas.

In the printer's fonts from which this book is made there are few figures among the types, and we have no design to make it a guide-book of our journey, nor to garnish its pages by statistics of products or population. It is enough to say that these combined cities, whose site thirty years ago was nameless, have now a population of one hundred and sixty thousand, with many railroads, great mills of every kind, and a business and social life having scant trace of pioneer days and ways. There are surprising beauties in the outskirts of the cities, in fair lakes set round with winding roads overgrown with trees and vines, and some historic spots whose natural beauties have received the new enchantments that legend and poetry give.

Westward now, straight as the arrow flies, with hardly shadow of a turning till we cross the bar at the mouth of the Columbia, we are started on our two thousand mile railway ride!

The cars are neat and all the appointments elegant, and with the dining cars by day and the Pulman sleepers for the night, we need not make our pilgrimage a penance.

The country through Western Minnesota is half familiar, for it is a land of lakes and forests such as we have seen at home. At Brainerd there is excitement, for a local worthy, one Jack O'Neill, is dead, and "the boys" are giving him the honor of the best funeral the town affords. His life has not been one of unmixed virtue, for he died possessed of a dance-house and two saloons, was "lively with his gun," and not one but many times had "killed his man." But memories are short in the presence of the dead, and the Brainerd boys cannot miss the opportunity of improving the occasion. The procession is in progress as the train comes in; the municipal police, three in number, with silver stars and locust clubs, all the coaches that the town affords are here, with a motley following of wagons of varied kinds, and a showy hearse attended by a band. So the ex-saloonist is being gathered to his fathers.

In the early morning we cross the Red River and are in the Territory of Dakota. How wonderful it is in its illimitable magnitude! For three hundred miles due west we shall journey on its soil, and see in these pioneer homes the beginning of the splendid empire that is to be.

No richer soil lies out-doors than this of the Red River valley, and the subsequent journey across the continent shows no land so rich. The river is a sluggish creek, but it is navigable for the rude stern-wheelers northward for many miles. There is but little poetry of pleasant winding paths along its banks, for they are bare of trees except scattered cottonwoods. Fargo is a thriving city of ten thousand people, with electric lights and all the things that make a city in these modern times. The great bonanza farms are here, and it was these that gave impetus to Fargo. We pass the Dalrymple farm, with its great stacks and wide-extended buildings. The farm is estimated to contain seventy-five thousand acres, and the profits in 1882 from the twenty-seven thousand acres under cultivation were upwards of two hundred thousand dollars. Large towns are left behind; stations now are hardly more than stopping-places; here and there a solitary pre-emptor's cabin rises on these billowy plains, and about it are little signs of life, —

> "The first low wash of waves, where soon
> Shall roll the human sea."

There is a strange fascination in these unfenced plains; the sky makes such perfect circle of the horizon as one observes at sea; far backward even to the sky, forward too into the sky beyond, the iron path trails on its limitless length without a break; little *buttes* or hills dot the landscape, and narrow streams fringed with the cotton-wood, which of all the trees is the only one loyal to the plains. The fields are not absolutely level, but swelling in gentle undulations, with such variety of outline that one travels across

Dakota without weariness of seeing, every sense held captive by the fascination of

> "These gardens of the desert,
> The unshorn fields, boundless and beautiful,
> For which the speech of England has no name,—
> The prairies."

The land grows bare as we move westward from the Red River, though nowhere do we find it poor, according to our New England standard; the crops give only partial promise. The passengers are few, made up of tourists,— not many going across the continent, the forward car being filled with emigrants seeking homes.

At Bismarck, four hundred and twenty miles from St. Paul, we find the newly selected site of the capital of the Territory. It is a city, as things go here, but has failed to catch the boom it has desired, until now, selected as the place of legislation, the thrifty citizens wait for the coming of the expected multitudes. It has a population of three thousand five hundred, but is limitless in expectations. In the Land Office that we visit, the city that is to be is marked upon the map with metropolitan dimensions, with squares and parks, great blocks, and avenues leading into space. The stores are large in superficial surface on the street, but apt to disappoint behind the wide-extended fronts; and these frail houses which, covered with no hypocrisy of paint, so show the grain of the native pine can hardly give much comfort when the blizzards come.

We have no thought of purchase here, for we are no incognito millionnaires; but upon the sidewalk a seedy-looking, landless native spies us, and comes up with friendly warning against the land-sharks of the place. To soften his revilings we mildly ask, "Is not the land here good?" when he turns upon us with such contempt as the "tender-foot" merits from the natives, and contemptuously answers, "Good! why, man, it won't make mud!" The Missouri River is a mile beyond, spanned by a million-dollar bridge. The river is simply a vast mud-puddle in motion, with great flats and meadows covered with marshy grass sifted full of sand; the shores are bluffy, but unattractive; and the voyage to Fort Benton, a thousand miles beyond, on these rude steamers here, does not form an outlook sufficiently alluring to make us tarry for the long *détour*.

Fort Lincoln is close in sight upon the bluff, with many associations of recent Indian wars and the brave Custer, who was stationed here. The rival city, Mandan, is on the river's western side, — hardly in sight of it, but far enough away to miss the risings of the current in the days of freshet. It has a depot in the Queen Anne style, and such a hotel as we have nowhere found since we left the "Nicolett" at Minneapolis. A little park is beside the track, and the repair-shops of the road are here. It has the favor of the railway, and on this is built the expectations of the future. The city is between two rivers, for the Heart is just beyond; it is a county seat, and its population has doubled in the year. In 1879 the Indians had encampment here, the Sioux and Arickarees having then a pitched battle. It is only a two-year-old town, but has a public hall, a lyceum course, and the inevitable brace of rival papers. The main street is lined with stores, and only with difficulty — because of the swarming crowds — can we find passage on the sidewalks. The land slopes up to a high bluff, on which, in vision, doubtless every merchant now can see the shapely house he will inhabit when the millennium that is coming is fully come.

Mandan has peculiarly interesting prehistoric relics. An old cemetery has been found near by, containing the bones of a giant race; mounds filled with stone weapons, arrow heads, rude pottery, vases of flints and agates. The pottery is delicately finished, and decorated with much artistic skill. The mounds are not simply the treasure-chests of a vanished race, but catacombs of the dead. Skeletons of men and horses rest here in shrouds of ashes; and though the Indians have tenacious memories, and preserve traditions of the dead for ages, yet they have no legends coming down from older tribes of this race buried here, and they call these "spirit mounds," filled with relics of a shadowy people.

We may be pardoned if we linger here at Mandan longer than is our custom in our westward flight, for why should not our heart be where our treasure is? Yes, we are owners of Mandan soil! This is the fashion in which it happens: We are writing in the office of the "Inter-Ocean;" the Professor paces close beside us, impatient for his bed. A young man enters and claims acquaintance with him on the ground that he once slept beneath his teachings in the class-room. The young man has a land office in the town, and as it is yet some short of midnight, and we are to leave upon the morning train, he invites him down to see the good fortune he has acquired.

In an hour's time a messenger comes back with summons from the Professor, and in an office with great maps spread over his extended knees we find him seriously meditating a purchase in the town. The Professor is a man mature in years; not greatly given to foolish speculation, nor so affluent in purse that he can greatly hinder the advent of actual settlers by his speculative dissipations. We try beneath the map to nudge him into caution, making pleasantly satirical remarks about buying city lots in a town scarce weaned as yet; but the Professor has the mania on, and feeling that it would be a shabby thing to desert a friend, we buy the lots adjoining those selected by the learned pundit, that we may throw our tomato-cans over the Professor's fence, and also absorb such wisdom as comes from close proximity to the home where a wise man lives.

We put the agent on his honor, and are assured — for he seems to be an honest man — that in a year, at least, the lots will double; and though we offer then and there to sell them back for just a third above the cost, and save the trouble of a deed, yet his refusal does not shake our faith, and our Mandan lots, half through the summer, by reason of the profit they will bring, give reason for every folly that depletes the hoard hidden in our inner pocket for the trip. We walk out in the moonlight to see the purchase we have made: we find the place where the boulevard will be on which our lots face so pleasantly upon the map, and though the bluff on which they rest is somewhat distant, and there is no sign of habitation within a mile at least, and though the city seems to be growing east instead of west, yet we have somewhere heard that every city at last grows on its westward side, and that the star of empire westward goes in the direction of our lots. So we find comfort, in the moonlight, looking at our land, though, to be fair and square, we have no other hint of where it is, beyond the general fact that it is somewhere between the track and the Canadian line.

Six hundred miles or more from St. Paul, and

we roll off the prairie into the "Bad Lands," which extend on either side of the Little Missouri River through a belt of forty miles. It is a region of desolation, softened by spots of tender beauty. Great *buttes* of clay seamed with gulches, fields compared with which the dreariest desert is beautiful; bluffs scarred with such washings as the storms may give; vast amphitheatre-like spaces; the broken, colorless soil walled around with hills carved into such fantastic sculpturings as a race of giant goblins might fashion.

There are wondrous colors here: great *buttes* girdled with yellow bands, and bright vermilion patches set against the neutral tints of this weird, spectral land. The very grass is wiry, as though made of steel, covering the fields which have softened into vegetation with such decoration as the frost rime makes upon a winter's day. On horseback from the Little Missouri station we ride out over these Bad Lands, and look down into such depths of desolation as we have never seen before: scoriæ, petrified wood, and fossil leaves are everywhere; mountains of lignite burning in perpetual flames, the great seams sulphur-crested; everywhere fantastic peaks, monuments set in goblin petrifactions,—such is this "Pyramid Park," as yet almost unknown here in Dakota. The Professor tells us that this region was once the bed of a great lake, out of whose richness grew luxuriant vegetation. This passed away, and, pressed by succeeding growths, transformed itself into vast beds of lignite coal, which, being without cementing ingredients, remained soft, and easily was washed by rains. The wear and wash of the varied strata under the action of rain and frost were very great. Hence " the little watercourses have curiously furrowed and corrugated sides," while the burning coal fuses the over and under lying beds, leaving the richly colored slag, and, as the veins burn out, great pits of desolation where the earth has sunk.

The day of our explorations is well suited to this sombre weirdness of landscape, for although it is in midsummer, the cold hail falls, and the wind, whistling around the *buttes*, chills us to the marrow. Our stopping-place is in an abandoned fort, converted, now that the soldiers have moved on, into a tourist's inn. It is the centre of a great stock-raising enterprise recently set on foot by the Marquis de Mores, a retired officer, now under temporary cloud in the Mandan jail because of his killing one Riley Luffcey, a local citizen. The young parson, who preaches in the old messroom on the Sabbath evening that overtakes us here, conducted the burial service. He tells us that in the annals of the settlement no man has died as yet outside his boots, which fact does not greatly cheer us, as in the old fort we close our eyes to sleep.

The Montana boundary line is passed, a pair of

antlers nailed upon a pole marking the place, and reaching soon the Yellowstone, for upwards of three hundred miles we pass up its pleasant valley. The stream has large proportions, and carries its clear waters over a stony bed; the mountains which flank the Rockies bring their snowy crests in view; little camps of strolling Indians have their colored tepees beside the track; the cowboy from the cattle-ranges becomes a familiar sight; the country now has legends of recent Indian battles; and through thriving towns, in sight of fairer mountains, we come to Bozeman, where we shall leave for a time our westward course, that we may view the wonders of the great Yellowstone Park.

On the omnibus which bears us to the village, a quarter of a mile away, we see in the driver one whom we used to know as a thriving merchant in the Empire State, while on the steps an undergraduate of Yale, as he stretches out his hand for fare, answers our remonstrance with the significant remark, "I know, gentlemen, it is something of a swindle to ask fifty cents for a five-cent ride, but it is the custom of the country," and — we find it is.

# THE YELLOWSTONE PARK.

*This masquerade
Of shape and color, light and shade.*
                                    WHITTIER.

## CHAPTER II.

### THE YELLOWSTONE PARK.

AT ten o'clock on a perfect summer day we turn our leaders' heads southward from the town of Bozeman for our long journey through the Yellowstone Park. Only yesterday we reached the town, and since then an outfit has been hired, stores and camping equipage procured, and the expedition fitted out. Our conveyance is a Studebaker wagon with three good seats, a canvas top, with wooden axles for the wheels, and heavy brake for the steep pitches of the hills. Two heavy horses are at the pole, while two lighter ones, fit for saddle purposes, serve as leaders. We have provisioned heavily, for we shall find no stores along the way, carrying also forage for the horses, with tent and all conveniences for half a month of roughing it. Our driver is a genius in his way, "Toot" by name, although not christened by it, if ever he was christened. His name adorns no calendar of saints, although not half those ancient worthies had such nimble-witted tongue, nor hand so deft in all the arts of life in wonder-land. He swears at times with most provoking volubility; but his oaths are not the common sort, and Toot has lived for half his life upon the plains. He draws the long bow sometimes in the strange tales he tells us; but then he assures us he is not like other drivers in the Park, for when he tells the truth he is not ashamed to own it. In vain we try to put our jokes upon him; always he retorts to our discomfiture, and a more thoughtful, generous-hearted, rough-and-ready fellow never put foot upon a brake. He seems to like us, too, although we notice with just a touch of sadness that while he calls us pilgrims without one hint of bitterness, yet when he wishes to put the climax on the list of nouns with which he curses the stumbling nigh-side wheeler, he always adds, as the final curse, the word "pilgrim," which thing we do not like. His brother "Al" is with us, too, somewhat jaded, he tells us, with over-conviviality behind the bar of the saloon he keeps in Bozeman, going with us on the trip to try and taper off, although, to tell the truth, in two good weeks of observation we cannot see where the tapering comes in. He is, however, a ready-handed fellow, with native shrewdness much sharpened by an adventurous life, and at the camp-fire or on the long stretches of the road he makes the hours seem short with the story of his life.

The Professor is elated, for we are going towards wonder-land, and he has absorbing passion for freaks of nature and curious forms of rock and stone, with open ear, too, for every touch of humor, and open-hearted for the loveliness there is in nature. The Dramatic Critic and the Reporter sit beside each other, hilarious over the eternal picnic we have entered on; and thus equipped, passing beside the Chinese graveyard, where Toot tells us he has often feasted on the chicken left by pious friends upon the graves, we go southward towards the mountains which wall in the scenes which we have come so far to see.

The load is heavy, for the springs lie flat upon the axles; and while beyond Fort Ellis and over the heavy roads we journey, we may briefly tell something of the place towards which our leaders' heads are pointed.

In the Territory of Wyoming, in the northwestern portion, a tract of land, larger in area than Rhode Island and Delaware combined, by act of Congress, has been set apart for a national park. Nature here has gathered her masterpieces. Mountains tipped with eternal snows, forests, glens, and waterfalls, cañons colored with such rare tints as eye has never seen, springs and rivers of boiling water, geysers, mud springs, lakes, mineral forests, flowers, all that eye can wish is here. All this is preserved as the people's pleasure place; no devastating hand can despoil, no ranchman here shall feed his flock, nor farmer turn his furrow. The roads are rude as yet, and in the journey of three hundred miles or more that we shall make we shall find no hint of village, hardly the dwelling-place of human soul.

The first day of such a journey, however commonplace, abounds with incident, for every faculty is all alert, — even so trivial a thing as the setting of the tire beside the road, wrapping it with canvas after the manner of the plains, delights; while the long file of soldiers with dusty horses, returning from escorting General Sherman through the Park; the cattle feeding on the ranches; the shifting wonders of mountain, plain, and river; the camp at evening; the innumerable incidents along the way, — make pleasant the two days' journey to the Park.

We have no word of censure for those who have delayed the road, for no iron horse on iron rails could make such royal journey as this of ours. Every hour the mountains seem clothed in rarer hues, and across the fords of rivers, camping at night beside streams flowing over grassy beds, riding beneath cliffs fitly named "Cinnabar," and over streams so noisy that the name "Hell Roaring Creek" seems not out of place; up and over great passes, with the river foaming far below; through pleasant fields and glens, with crags and peaks and every form of nature that human vision can delight in, — so we come onward to the Park.

Human enterprise is quite alive just here, and, anticipating that the terminus of the road would make a place of business, thrifty fellows had made at Gardiner a veritable city. The Dramatic Critic takes the census of the town, and reports thirty-two houses, and twenty-eight of them saloons. As we return we notice at the post-office, which is the city's social centre, an absence of the ancient worthies we have seen before, to learn that they are in attendance on a "claim" meeting; for gold, they tell us, has been found the day before, though in the pans they show us we confess we cannot see the "color" of which they speak, and much suspect that they are trying to boom the town.

Four miles beyond and we are in the Park, and beneath us are the Mammoth Hot Springs. In the centre of the little valley is rising the great hotel of the Park Improvement Company, and on a little hill beyond the unpretentious house of the government superintendent. Beyond this, on either side, are thickly wooded hills, and on the east great mountains steep of ascent, like the walls of Webster from the Crawford Notch.

For acres here the soil is spread with sinter, the deposit from the boiling springs, white, with slight shade of yellow, most glaring to the eyes. Standing sentinel in this great desolation are monuments of sinter, the Giant's Thumb and Liberty Cap, forty feet and more in height; and then back, rising in terraces, are the famous springs. For two good miles or more above, the springs commence overflowing into pools, with great plateaus acres wide between, then flowing down and down in terrace-like descents to the valley's base. They are of every form: round like bowls, semicircular like balconies, with scalloped rims and corrugated sides. Some of these bowls are veritable cauldrons with seething waters; in others the water lies smooth as a mirror's face, rich in color and pleasant to the taste. It has magic power, for along the rims of these countless pools there are most exquisite decorations. The frost-work of a winter's window has not more dazzling wonders, delicate fretted work, flowers with rarest petals, curious lace-work fashionings, and finer weavings, as though a spider's web had stiffened into rock; with coralline traceries and quaint arabesques, as though this were the fairy's workshop, and we had surprised them at their toil. The color, too, is marvellous. The prevailing tint is salmon, but shading into every hue, with such invisible transitions as the colors of a rare sea-shell; and there are great bands of red and brown and creamy filaments floating in the water. In the St. Lawrence, just outward from the entrance-way to the Lake of the Thousand Islands, there is a great field of water vegetation. The water lies not many feet above the bottom, and beneath are such marvels of marine growth as we have never elsewhere seen; flowers and weeds, delicately veined leaves and twining vines, richer because, like a Claude Lorraine glass, the transparent water adds its graces. But here are greater marvels, flowers of finer petals and richer hued; and the grace of form is not in our deceptive vision, for beneath our microscopes even fairer wonders are revealed. These things are creations of the water, from it they receive their beauty and by it they exist; and when the gentle tide recedes, these fair wonders change to the white sinter's dust.

The living springs are numberless,— an area of one hundred and seventy acres is covered by them,— while the deposit left by the flowings of ages occupies an area of three square miles. But backward even into the forests a mile beyond are extinct springs, dry caverns, with spectral trees half buried with the sinter's dust, and Stygian caves emitting deadly fumes, and inland lakes set round with marvels, and walling in the great wonder-place are hills set thick with foliage.

We push onward now, for in our explorations we can only touch and go; but we will not push with speed, for we are climbing Terrace Mountain, and in the two miles' ascent we must lift ourselves three thousand feet. The road is beautiful with forest scenes; great reaches of sunlight leading into distant shade, and craggy rocks all draperied with moss, and such pleasant odors as the woods distil.

A dead bear lies beside the road, and our driver tells us that we must keep good guard to-night at our camp close by. The road winds on in pleasant ways until, twelve miles beyond the springs, we come to the Obsidian Cliffs. These are basalt cliffs one thousand feet in length, perhaps two hundred feet in height, and are of pure volcanic glass. It is a mountain of jet, black, brilliant, hard as flint. It is literally a glass road over which we journey; for Beaver Lake is just below, and the cliff runs its roots into the waters. Pick and drill have no power here, and only by building huge fires upon the rocks and breaking them by water poured upon the heated stone, could the road be made.

Nine miles beyond, we stop for lengthy exploration of the Norris Geyser Basin. We are in the geyser region now, and out of the forest. Leaving our team to meet us later, we enter upon what seems to be a frozen sea. For miles around there is the sinter's desolation, with no relief for dazzled eyes save here and there a geyser's intermittent flow, and the green woods beyond. On the edges just where the woods come down are springs, and mud-pots seething, — boiling springs, and great cauldrons horrible to see. From the overlooking hill we survey the scene. No nightmare vision ever pictured desolation so great. Sahara's plains are soft and beautiful compared to this; for there, is no malignity, but here, is desolation most complete, and added to it, in these steaming cauldrons, the spouting geysers, the dark venomous-looking mud-pots with their seething mass of variegated clay, there is active hate. The very soil beneath our feet is but a shell,—a frozen scum above a cauldron's waters; and fissures yawn at us, and the thin crust bends, and from crack and seam come scream and hiss, as though in subterranean caverns vipers scented the coming of human prey.

The desolation is oppressive; the air is noisy with escaping steam from "Steamboat Vent," which is a huge cavern sending forth terrific roar; and though there are emerald pools holding purest water in royal vessels, and sulphur crystals yellow as beaten gold, yet the scene is fearful in its vast unrelieved malignant weirdness. The "Minute Man" is a spouting geyser here, throwing steam some thirty feet in height each minute, while the larger "Monarch" once a day sends out a torrent of one hundred feet. Coming through the forest now, three miles or more, we descend into Elk Park, one of the pleasant places of which this great domain is full. It is almost circular in form, rimmed round with pleasant hills, thick-covered with foliage. A tiny spiral of steam rising in the woods beyond is all the token given that this is the geyser region. Beyond this it is as though a little English vale in Sussex had been transported here; and just beyond the town of Ripon, where the old path winds over the hills on its meandering way to Fountains Abbey, the fairest ruins in Europe, there is a scene like this. The grass is wild, but it has the pleasant lawn-like green of fields long mellowed by human culture; and by such graceful slopings does it approach the hills, and by such gentle, lover-like approaches do the hills bend down to meet the fields, and so proudly rise the peaks that sentinel the valley, that, coming from the geysers yonder, entrance here is like the merging of a sleeper's nightmare into a peaceful dream.

There is no sight of human habitation, no creature pastures in these fields, bright with ten thousand flowers; like all the region, it is a solitude, save only the Gibbon River, which flows along beside our wheels with sluggish flow.

Into the Gibbon River Cañon we enter now. The river has roused with sudden passion, and fights its way along with tumult. Two thousand feet above us the walls rise up, scarred by frost and storm, yet decked with ferns and grasses, where the rock has softened into soil. And there are pleasant things along the way, — great bowlders in the stream, with trees like plumes upon them, and translucent springs, and boiling ones beside the way, and winding ways along the bank, and sharp pitches downward to the river, and long reaches of wheeling in the stream hugging the cliff, and perilous fords, where wonder is alive as to whether the waters will submerge the wheels.

There is no lovelier forest road than this; for the air is resinous, and there are rare surprises of cliff and forest, and the road winds on in gentle curvatures, while our wheels run noiselessly over the rich brown needles of the pine. Right in the heart of the forest is the Gibbon River Falls; the descent is perilous, for the way is steep, and the walls of the river go down by sheer descent into a vast gulf. The falls are not wonderful here, but in New England would be justly famous.

The settings are incomparable; for the chasm has grand sweeping lines, and the rock has no trace of any pity in fern or flower, but is stern and pitiless in its neutral tints, saying to us, if it speaks at all, that this is stern work, standing here for ages in the wilderness to guard this torrent.

Out of the very heart of the hills the river comes; it takes its momentary leap, and, flecked with foam, moves out of the awful chasm again into the eternal shadows.

The sun sets everywhere, but seldom with such rare colorings as tint the heavens now, as with hurrying wheels for the night's encampment, crossing the Divide through such a spectral forest as Doré paints for the journeys of the "Wandering Jew," we tether our horses beside the Firehole River. It is a weird place. The river fed by the geysers has hardly cooled as yet, and when the great camp-fire is kindled, there are most uncanny shadows here. There is a strange witchery in this camping-place. The wind has most peculiar wail and moan; the camp-fire never before so transformed our little company. And why is it that to-night our guides, with such rare embellishments of fancy, tell of old fights with the Sioux and Pawnees? All through the night the strange wind sighs above us; beyond, the Stygian river flows without a sound; the camp-fire with its dying flames makes strange shadows till the dawn, while through the night the stealthy trampings in the forest seem to come from other beasts than those that draw us on our journey.

Only a few miles beyond we come to the Middle Geyser Basin. The local name is "Hell's Half Acre;" well bestowed, for here is the great Excelsior Geyser, the largest in the world. Looking down into it, it seems to be the crater of hell, two hundred feet in width, with jagged walls, and such terrific masonry as infernal spirits might have laid. The cauldron bubbles, seethes, and steams, giving no hint that twice a day it sends forth a stream of water that is a river sixty feet in diameter, and from sixty to three hundred feet in height. The little channels which carry constantly the drainage of the geyser are rare in beauty, being lined with delicate silken laminæ of wondrous color, shading from white to rose, mauve, and scarlet.

Behind this geyser, upward toward the hills, is the Grand Prismatic Pool. These other things are wonderful, and this whole region is the wonder-land; but here, unless there is some unwonted sorcery in the atmosphere of this summer's day, is the most beautiful thing the whole round earth carries on its bosom, — a pool of water three hundred feet in width, deep in its central part, but shallow like the sea where it touches the shore. The water is simply marvellous in beauty. A thousand rainbows must be dissolving here; for from the central blue wondrous tints of emerald, sapphire, beryl, topaz, orange, green, yellow, all intermingle, — not simply dead color, but brilliant, flashing like polished gems. This comes from no enchantment of the sun; from every point the beauty is the same; and though we climb into the forest, and look down between the branches, even then the great pool lies in the sun, like a vision of the celestial city. The settings of this wondrous thing are worthy of it. Its walls are carved, as no sculptor's chisel ever cut, with strange garlandings of leaf and flower, and rare enamellings, with silken filaments underneath concealing, yet revealing, fairer beauties.

The Turquoise Pool, on a lower level, to one who will study its attractions, may almost dispute the supremacy with the more brilliant beauty just above. It is one hundred feet across, with irregular outline, having on its outer rim, where the water does not come, only the common sinter; but just below, where the magic water touches, there are delicate enamellings, fawn-colored, changing into rings of every hue, with the ever-present mineral flowers that these waters love spread in bounty everywhere. The water is translucent, and down into great depths it goes. The walls below are white like alabaster, but strangely veined like agate. Great projecting walls come out, broken into craggy summits, like tiny mountain ridges; and there are winding roads against the cliffs, and little walls built upon the outer side, and marble bridges stained as though with age; and underneath them torrents flow, and if one but had the finer vision, he would see, no doubt, armies winding up and down, and naiads looking at them from the peaks above: into all curious things this pool is broken, — caves and peaks, faint hint of castles, so marvellously has Nature wrought.

Six miles above, fifty miles southward from the entrance of the Park, the geyser region culminates in the Upper Basin. This place contains four square miles, and within an area of half a mile is the greatest geyser region in the world. The surface is irregular, rising in ridges from the river, and on these are the multitude of geysers and boiling springs. It is not easy to compute their number. There are at least twenty geysers of great size, with many others of lesser fame. They have built up a kind of collar around their orifices of geyserite, — hard, smooth, delicately tinted. Some of these in the older ones are great mounds, others small; some with but one orifice, others, like the grotto, with many. The interval between the eruptions varies from one hour to fourteen days, the height of the stream also varying from twenty to two hundred feet. The geysers change from time to time, — old ones becoming extinct, new ones breaking out in other places. They are of every form, from a plain cone to great fantastic grottos. The form of their flowing varies: some flow in a constant, even, symmetrical flow; others, in great spurts.

As we enter the basin, the Castle is rumbling with terrific violence. The water has just ceased, but for an hour at least there will be the sound of the subsiding agitation. During our stay many others throw their stream, awing us with the majesty of their terrific power. One wonders here and is silent. He feels that there is a power slumbering beneath his feet, compared with which human strength is weakness; and stay he longer or shorter time, he never learns to become familiar with these vast forces imprisoned here.

We pitch our tent among these things, and watch

and wonder. Once an hour Old Faithful throws its stream a good hundred feet, — beautiful by day as the fountains of Versailles; but when the moonlight falls at night, what pen can tell the story of its loveliness?

# SAUNTERINGS IN WONDER–LAND.

*To-morrow to fresh woods and pastures new.*
LYCIDAS.

## CHAPTER III.

### SAUNTERINGS IN WONDER-LAND.

BACKWARD on our track, ten miles or more, we must come to the forks of the Firehole before we branch eastward to the lake thirty miles away. The Madison Divide lies across the way, and, by long and tedious ascent, must be crossed. The way is through the forest now. Over the summit, dropping down a little, we come to Mary's Lake, a little mountain tarn, set round with woods. Pleasant alternations of woods and fields now follow; and when we reach the Hayden Valley, and for hours wind over its rolling fields, we find that we have come upon another phase of the strangely varying scenery of this wonder region. Little bits of exquisite landscape come in view, picturesque woodland scenes, with great rolling sweeps of verdure, bounded by the Washburn range, at whose feet is the crowning wonder of waterfall and gorge. Our camp at night is beside the Black Foot Creek, just in the fringes of the woodland where pasturage grows rank, and wood and water, the essentials of a camp, are found.

The wagon road now winds on around the shoulders of little *buttes* which dot the Park; but in the clear morning air — being on horseback now — we can make straight passage towards the distant river, having time in our solitary journey to catch the full glory of this rare morning light, and see, unvexed by sound of wheel or human voice, the pleasant things along the way. There is, too, a slight hint of trail, and, even if we lose the course, we have but to go upon the summit of these little peaks to see the wagon winding on its way. It is a balmy air, and over Italy never brooded a fairer sky than this. The trail has curious windings, and the grass is brilliant with many flowers. We know not whether, in the high altitudes, it is because the flowers are nearer to the sun that they have unwonted color, but nowhere is there such a field of cloth of gold as on the Alps, not half a mile on the south side of the very summit of the Simplon Pass; and no florist's garden ever had such royal blue and yellow star-shaped flowers, as these that lie here looking at the sun.

We are in the valley now, and in steady, even rise the fields slope upward to the forests, which come down in little points, with pleasant pasture-lands between, running up beneath the branches into turf made brown with the needles of the pines. An elk with branching antlers is striding on, just beyond our bullet's range, if we had heart to kill; and across a river ford we now go upward into groves, not dense nor large, but such shady places as fringe the old pastures on the New England hills. The flowers only follow us to the borders of the woods; but there are lights and shadows dancing here, and such sweet balsam odors as intoxicate. We are eight thousand feet above the sea, but there is no sign of stunted vegetation. The road dips downward into pleasant valleys, then on again between the trees, the great ranges coming into vision on the summits. The solitude is absolute; no cattle pasture here; no smoke from any home; no sound of bird nor insect, — nothing save the low sweet whispering of the pines, wondering to each other why this stranger has come to break their solitude. As we descend the hill, the great river comes in view. It is a lordly thing; how broad it is! green as Niagara, and swift as the "arrowy Rhone"! While descending a little on the river's bank, in the progress of our journey, we look down into the river just where an indentation of the shore makes a little bay of quiet water, and there we count more than thirty trout, good fourteen inches long, we know; and this can be relied upon, because we are no fisherman, and have not that infirmity of conscience which makes an angler incapable of probity when speaking of a fish.

We have a friend at home who has always much annoyed us by speaking of the monster fish he catches, and simply that we may overtop our friend's romancings, we throw a fly into the stream, and (to be fairly honest) in less than forty seconds we land two of these monsters.

We are going up the river now, and just where the lawn-like fields merge in the forest, opens wide the great lake we have come so far to see. We have large payment for our pains. It is something wonderful to think that if Mount Washington were sunk within these waters, down to the level of the sea, still the surface of the lake would be half the mountain's height above its summit. It has an area of some one hundred and fifty miles or more, in shape not unlike the open palm, with such extensions of bay and inlet as the fingers make upon the hand. The color is intensely brilliant, a bright sapphire blue. Did we dare to draw its outlines, we should say that on the northern side there is a long bluffy shore, with trees of fir and pine, terminating near the waters in pleasant pasture-lands, which catch and hold the evening light. Back of these is the great Wind River range, most rugged peaks, with gnarled and seamy sides. The lake flows round out-jutting points, and then stretches out its sapphire arms in great reaches till it touches a rough wall of stone, which, if the intervening twenty miles do not deceive us, is a mountain, reaching up ten thousand feet or more, till it finds its thatch of eternal snow. Southward moving upon the other side, and there great tongues of mountains push into the lake, backed by twin peaks, which seem to be within speaking-distance of each other, but may be forty miles away. Coming nearer, we find a gentler mountain, which has so yielded to milder influences that it has permitted the warm fir-trees to clothe it. The old barbaric temper is not all civilized out of it, for there is just one touch of snow hanging defiant still upon its front. And now far southward, with only a low arm of land, thick-wooded, and with perhaps another arm of the lake behind it, looms up the grand old Teton range, not serrated like the mountains on the other side, but broad-flanked and snow-crowned.

There is an island lying midway in the lake, having, we know, fair scenes, if only there was boat of any kind upon the lake. The shores upon the western side slant down in pleasant beaches, covered thick with rare obsidian glass, petrified wood, jasper, chalcedony, with little ridges of shining sand, black as ink, and windrows of pebbles mixed with stones of brilliant hue. The Yellowstone Lake is scarcely known, and yet it can but be the case that it is soon to take its place among the world's famous lakes. The English lakes, without their associations, are not so fair as this. Loch Lomond is a fadeless picture; but the rare sunset which changed its waters into a lake of amethyst belongs not to it, and only once in a thousand years can it be illuminated with such glory as transfigured it before our adoring eyes. Maggiore is matchless in the placidity of its waters, with the Alps towering over them, with shores garlanded with traceries of vine and thicket; but it is a painted sea of dreams, and these islands are made by hand of man rather than the work of God. Como is beautiful beyond expression; to describe its beauties by common prose is profanation, — only poetry or music can picture Como with its waters winding in among the encircling hills, and its marble villas peeping out from groves of fig and lustrous veil of vine. But Como is a river rather than a lake, lacking strength, as do all these southern lakes. They are beautiful, but strength and beauty must be joined in bridal bonds to make the perfect scene. Lake Geneva in Switzerland, and our own Lake George, are hardly fairer than this almost unknown lake of wonder-land. Geneva is grander in proportions, the mountains slope in fairer lines, and there are terraced vineyards, and the inimitable charm that history and poetry give; but this lake has larger breadth, and we do not think that even Geneva's waters ever have such rare brilliancy of hue; while the mountains of Lake George, fair as they are in their great burly massiveness, lack the royal crown of these eternal snows.

Five miles beyond, backward from the lake, by pleasant forest trail, we find the Natural Bridge, a span of thirty feet, thrown in shapely arch one hundred feet above the stream.

There is some human interest here in our camp beside the lake, for there is coming now out of the forest the shaggy-bearded ranger whom two hours ago we met far back upon the Colorado trail. He has driven his twenty horses for five months thus through the wilderness from the far southern country; and later on we hear that he has stolen them from an Indian whom he murdered. At any rate, he is most shy of speech, keeping note of passing days by the notched stick hanging at his belt, and driving in the brood, — the little colts born on the journey through the woods, — the herd led on by a sorrel leader with a tinkling bell.

We have neighbors now making camp beside us on the bluff above the lake. A sick man, in a rude log cabin, has spent the summer here, coming from his distant home, cheated with delusive hope that this pure air might build again his broken lungs; the librarian of Yale College is in the adjoining camp, most deft of hand in all the service of this gypsy life; and when the night comes on, and the great camp-fire burns, we send invitation to our neighbors to come and visit us, and so we sit and talk beside the fire, — the Professors, of the wonders of the region; old tourists, of routes of travel; the younger men and women, of other things, we guess, so soft and tender are their whisperings; the ranger on the other side looking on in silence; while the great lake just down the bluff lies rippleless and beautiful in the moonlight of a perfect night.

It is fifteen miles or more to the crowning glory of this wonder-land, the Great Gorge of the Yellowstone. We are on horseback now, and may take the trail, which carries us through denser woods and over higher summits than the wagon road, with slighter chance of disturbance of the solitude in which we wish to worship in this fair temple. We have stood in vestibule and aisle, but now we are approaching the altar where culminates the glory of the holy place. Most leisurely we journey in the winding paths, the air fragrant with the distillations of the pines, with glimpses of the river from the hills, and little fords from which we drink, bending from our saddles; a sulphur mountain is beside the road, and there are pleasant pasture paths which seem like the sunny slopes of the familiar New England hills. We see no human being on the way, nor any cattle feeding; no living thing, except in one of the great streams whose waters touch our saddle-girths great pelicans stand watching us. But now the river is in angry mood; in great waves it frets and storms and battles with the rocks along its way; for we have found the rapids, and just beyond the little glen set round with trees, where rises the smoke of our encampment, is the Yellowstone's Upper Falls. From the overtopping rock we may look down a hundred feet or more into the great chasm, where the rainbow lies amid the mist. There are stern rocks and bowlders here, which might appal us were they not so draperied with moss; while beyond, out of the mist and shadows, the river flows laughingly between its banks of green.

There is wanting little here to make the perfect picture, for the rapids are above, huge rocks midway in the stream divide the waters, and savage cliffs rise up on either side, covered with such decorations as the mist-fingers have placed in seam and crevice.

This wonder-land is poor in legendary lore, for the poet's wand has not yet called forth the stories of its past. There is, however, here just a touch of tragedy; for this chasm has been the tomb of brave men. Not many years ago, somewhere in this region, there was an outbreak of the tribe of Crow Indians. The settlers were massacred; and from the neighboring forts the troops came in to find atonement for the crime. A little band of braves, close pressed, came up the valley, and, weary with their flight, finding no rest nor hope of safety, halted here, resolved to die in good, brave fashion. They made a raft of fallen trees, gathcring them from the woods close by, and tying them together with wicker-work of branch and vine, brought it to the river, just on the rapids' edge above the falls. The pursuing soldiers came, with swift advancings, through the woods, and when on the little cliff above they halted to fire upon the fugitives, the rude raft was launched, bearing its savage freight. The soldiers fired upon the fated crew; the answering shot went back, the raft trembled on the brink, and then plunged into the abyss with dying brave and living warrior.

Not quite a mile beyond, with pleasant path between, over bridge of corduroy, in sight of cascade and grotto pools, we descend to the Lower Falls. We will go slowly down, because we have caught glimpse of the wonder-gorge, and cannot, without a pang of sadness, give up our loyalty to the falls behind, to which, not half an hour ago, we gave our heart.

We have seen the upper walls of the great chasm, bright like the western sky at close of day, but we will watch the descending path, and shut out the vision, till now we stand upon the platform at the falls, and raise our eyes to such a scene as no other spot on earth can give. Language is but a clumsy thing with which to paint the glories of this wonder-place. The richest pigments of artists of largest fame have failed; and while men have smiled at the flaming canvas, and said, "It is impossible," the baffled painter has grieved that his poor brush had failed to tell half the story of this exceeding loveliness. Behind us, as we stand upon the platform, are the quiet woods; the river narrows just above to eighty feet, and then with waters strangely green they plunge three hundred feet into the awful gulf. Niagara may leap twice as far as now, and hardly touch the stream below; and while there is not Niagara's majesty, and only slightest tithe of its massive volume, yet where does water ever fall with such incomparable loveliness as here? With steady hand clinging to the platform's rail, we will look down; later on, from yonder peak, we will lie for hours in the sun, and yield ourselves to the fascinations of this royal scene.

A great wall rises beside the falls; on the yonder side it seems to be of porphyry,—so is it colored, —but there is rare tenderness of hue, as though a rime spread over it; and there are touches, too, of softer nature in fern and moss, with little edgings of green enamel such as Nature loves to lay around the sharp edges of crack and seam. In great, majestic, even poise the water, all unbroken, flows out into the air, gathering soon in little folds of lace-like streams, then breaking into mist before it changes into smoke three hundred feet below.

There are sloping ledges down where the fall changes to a river, and behind the fall there are rocks curiously covered with dark grasses, as though draperied in a widow's weeds; and there are others green with moss, and stones uncovered, save where the mist condenses and the little rivulets run down. Half-way up, just where the volume of the water shades thinner toward the sides, the water breaks into rocket-like jets; beside the walls it is a mist-torrent, farther on a wreath of smoke, while from other points of vision the water seems like angels falling down, trailing veils of mist. Never did waterfall pour itself into such royal vessel; for the great gorge, rising from the river good two thousand feet, winds down eight miles or more.

Strip this wonder-gorge of all these banners that cover it; change it into bare walls of stone, walling in the silver ribbon at its base, and it is still marvellous; for on the eastern side it rises up in steep ascent, ridged with great protruding veins, shaped into stern promontory and projecting walls, with little hint of any pitying earth upon it, till up against the sky it breaks into woods and fields running back into the hills.

The western wall is made of softer stuff, and snows and torrents — the hungry teeth of winter frosts — have sculptured here such marvels as only those whose eye has seen will believe exist. Great columns, such as Titans might erect to celebrate victories, are here, and castles such as crown the Rhine, and gateways fit to sentinel the gardens of the gods; peaks and towers, buttresses and bastions, rugged fortress, Gothic arches, and cathedral spires, — such would be the gorge if we had no eye to see the outward glory spread on this anatomy of rock.

But the prism does not more dissolve the sun than do the walls catch and separate its glory. All the color which the sun in the ages has poured into the earth has been forced into these cliffs by the alchemy of the hot springs which make this wonder-land. The prevailing tint is yellow, but shading into lemon, orange, salmon, with great bands of white, changing by invisible transitions to softer shades of rose and pink. Far down the gorge there are great blotches of red and scarlet, jutting cliffs of cinnabar, with rare background of such rich yellow as the sinter makes. Such for eight miles is the gorge, broken into every variety of contour, bearing its silver river down with many windings, rising up in most majestic sweep, and so rich in its transcendent colorings, that one might feel that a rainbow spreading its arch had been shattered here, and left its colors on the cliffs, or that this is some old Moorish city decorated for a fête.

There are innumerable points of observation from these great projecting cliffs; each one reveals a changing picture; the path winds in and out, skirting the chasm, which drops down at times in sheer descent, and again slopes so gently that the rocks we roll go winding on the descending road for a good thousand feet before they find the precipice. Some half a mile down the gorge, just where the eye sees the falls as a noiseless sheet of spray, looking from the summit of the cliff, at least five hundred feet below, there stands a great monument, as solitary as Stylites' Pillar. On the summit of it, covering all its little surface, is an eagle's nest, made of coarsely braided branches; and all day long the great eagle soars over the gorge, making the solitude even more complete.

We have great desire to descend into the cañon, and from the river's brink look up. Nowhere do we find a place where it seems possible that human foot can find safe passage. But at last we find a watercourse, whose way we can seem to trace even to the river, although we know that the lower space may be so foreshortened that the little gaps far below may perhaps be great impassable reaches. With heavy clamberings over rock and bowlder we descend, until, finding every step fatiguing, we rise on the brook's wall, which goes down in a kind of ridge with somewhat gentle slope. We will go on by this until it terminates in the great Cinnabar Tower, which is one of the famous things within the gorge, and then we will descend its side into the stream again, and so go downward to the river. But the wall grows narrow, until, between us and the widening rock which leads on to the tower, there is only a narrow ridge not half a dozen feet in width. There is ample space for walking, if only the sloping walls did not descend so far, and we have no surety of steady nerves to keep us on the track; so, commencing back, we run across. We have come thus to the great cliff, brilliant-hued, square, massive, like some old mediæval fortress, and, climbing up with perilous toiling, we look down from its summit into the fearful chasm. Coming back a little, we descend into the bed of the brook, which we will follow to the river. The descent is hard; for the soil is only shaly rock, with only such security as roots of stunted trees, long dead, can give. We reach the stream, now dry in the summer's drought, cross over, when, lo! we find the river's course terminates in a precipice, so steep, that we can see no line of wall, so deep, that the river there seems almost as indistinct as from the summit yonder. We are not sorry, for the way is long behind us to retrace, and already the shadows gather in the gorge; but such is the fatal curiosity of man, that we desire to go at least to the very verge of the precipice, to see how far indeed the walls descend. We go with cautious clingings, until we are at the brink, just where the sloping bank goes downward to the edge.

There are three of us, and the most adventurous one, lying half-extended on the sloping bank, seeks to let himself down a little nearer, when suddenly he feels the shaly mass slide with him towards the gulf of horrors. He stretches out his hands, but the soil he clutches is in motion, and only when in another moment he must plunge over the fearful precipice does the moving mass stop its motion. So near is he to the brink, that his staff falls over from his grasp, and with bleeding hands he crawls back to safety.

We have slight heart now to continue exploration; with painful effort we gain the summit, trying, only with ill success, to laugh away remembrance of the peril we have passed. But at night in our little camp beside the rapids more than once we have vision of the towering cliff, and in our broken dreams feel the motion of the treacherous soil bearing us silently over the precipice into the gulf of death.

# A FIFTY-MILE WALK.

*Pacing through the forest,*
*Chewing the food of sweet and bitter fancy.*
                                        As You Like It.

## CHAPTER IV.

### A FIFTY-MILE WALK.

THERE is no road from the Lower Falls to the Mammoth Hot Springs except the one over which we have travelled. There is, however, a trail passable for foot travellers and saddle horses; and as there are many attractions along the way, the three younger members of the party conclude to take this trail, and meet the outfit on the third day at the springs, fifty miles away. We have brought saddles for our leaders for just this trip, and with the lightened load Toot tells us that he can make his time with the wheelers only. As one at best must walk, we conclude to make the trip on foot.

The nights are severely cold in these high latitudes, and without the shelter of a tent we shall have good need of covering; so in the preparations for the journey each takes a pair of blankets, with overcoat and gossamer, all deftly wrapped around the canned provisions that shall feed us. Even a pair of blankets and an overcoat make a fair-sized pack for a three days' summer march; but add to this several solid cans of provender, and it is not wonderful that at the start it pulls a little heavy on the straps, and before the walk is ended it weighs a ton at least.

Just above the Lower Falls the trail leads off, passing over pleasant hills, into the surprising park-like pastures which so abound in this wonder-region. The day is one of the rare days which sometimes in New England come in early autumn, when the air is balminess itself, and every leaf stands outlined in the sun. We stop for dinner at a pleasant brook, and, with such elation as children have, kindle our fire beside the stream and undo our packs. We find, with consternation, that we are wretchedly provisioned. In the hurry of our start each has selected what he deems his proportion of the outfit for the walk, and so, when our elaborately decorated cans are placed in line, we find that every one of us has chosen the "Boston Baked Beans" with which our outfit was liberally supplied. A solitary can of oysters alone varies the eternal monotony of beans, while the crackers, which at the start had filled the pockets of our coats, had been nibbled on the way, and, with only a slight residue of powdery crumbs, are gone.

A little piece of bacon, which somehow stews itself away into the blackest, crimpiest kind of substance, is the only meat we have provided; while the package that contains the tea we bring has broken in our pockets, in the exigencies of the morning walk, giving, in the subsequent stewings of the journey, a nondescript decoction of oolong, cracker-dust, and the frayed shoddy nap of our pocket linings. We have many friends in Boston. We have lived within sight of its gilded dome, and have often mused beside the Frog-Pond of its Common. We have never made invidious remarks about its crooked streets, sneered at its institutions, believed that a Boston native is simply "the east wind made flesh," nor cherished the heresy that one born in Boston has any need to be born again. But when we see here upon the grass beans to right of us, beans to left of us, and think that for two days and more we must feed absolutely on this plebeian diet, our hearts sink, and our tongue would keep unwonted silence should all the world rise to defame the " Modern Athens " !

We have no seasoning of any kind, nor spoon, nor knife,— nothing but unseasoned beans to be eaten with a wooden spoon. A bean is a kind of delusive thing, — it fills, but does not satisfy ; and this eating from the original package with a cedar-tasting wooden spoon, sweetening the unsavory meal with weak libations of a kind of crackery, pocket-lining flavored liquid, with no hint of sugar, milk, or any sweet disguisings, is getting back to nature to a degree we never have aspired to.

Filled, but not fed, we push on. The trail increases in the beauty through which it leads us. We are on the flanks of Dunraven Mountain, now going upward through pleasant woods. Long vistas open, and in the sun the perfect peaks stand clear and beautiful.

The trees run upward farther than we have ever seen on the New England mountains, and so broad of branch are they, that it seems as if an orchard from a New England farm had by some magic been hung here beneath the snows. There are such resting-places beside the little fords as the fairies might have chosen for their bathing-places, and for great spaces the trail winds through fields of flowers brilliant with the rich colorings of this rare region. The wild mustard changes the pasture slope into a field of the cloth of gold, with buttercups where the grass is closer woven, and blue gentians too, and in the woods delicate sprays of columbine and the rare Indian Plume, changing its hues from deep rich carmine to vermilion and magenta.

So we toil upward, the heavy packs borne easily because of the glory that lies along the way. Washburn has been in sight all through the day, separated from the trail by a foot-hill, itself a mountain. Our trail should lead over the summit of Mount Washburn, and when we find that the crest of the Divide is passed and we are leaving the mountain behind, we know that we have missed the diverging path. We go back a mile at least; but we do not find it, and forgetting that these mountains are not like the mountains we have been wont to climb, without longer searching for the trail we commence the ascent forthwith, making our own path as we go up. But we have forgotten the weight of our heavy packs and the exceeding rarity of the air upon these heights. For two hours at least we climb the foot-hill, with infinite weariness, only to find when on the summit, though we have crossed great drifts of snow, that we are at least two thousand feet below the peak of Washburn, and must descend into the valley a thousand feet before we can begin the ascent. The day is drawing on, and we are not fresh as in the morning; but there is the summit we have come to see, and see it we must before the darkness comes.

We rest long in the little valley far below. Arcadia never had sweeter place than this, with grass so green, and little streams so bright and musical, and such infinite sunniness, with no trace that ever human foot before had found its loveliness.

The summit seems miles away, and the ascent is more than steep. To simply raise ourselves to such a height would have appalled us once, but now we must carry these heavy packs, and make the journey in an atmosphere so rare that simple breathing is work enough.

At the very start, — for we are already eight thousand feet above the level of the sea, — our stages of progress are but brief; and as we climb, shorter and shorter are the journeys, until towards the summit, no matter how thoroughly we are rested, only twenty steps are needed to compel us to stop, panting, breathless, utterly exhausted, so tired that we dare not sit lest we may not be able to raise again the burden of our packs. For two hours we thus climb; conversation long since has ceased, for we have little breath to spare, and there is that semi-dizziness that comes with such exertions. Each one seeks the way that seems the easiest, and when we reach the narrow ridge we are far apart. Not yet is the summit found. There, five hundred feet above us, with yawning precipices on either side, stands the goal of our desires, with narrow, tortuous way between, rising above great gulfs of blackness and leading on round bowlders scarred with many storms. There is need of diligence of eye and foot, for we must swing ourselves around these cliff-like points, with only such protection as strong arms can get clinging to crack and crevice, our heavy packs hanging over awful chasms, seeking to pull us down to the great gulfs a thousand feet below. Even now we wonder whether it be possible to gain the summit and go downward to the timber line for camp before the darkness comes, and whether we shall not stop right here beneath the little shelter of the summit, and make our campfire of the bleached branches of the stunted firs, finding water in the melted snows. But we have heavy work before us on the morrow, and must have no dalliance here; and so, tightening strap and pack, we commence the final climb. It is a treacherous path, and only that no wind is blowing, and that we watch with utmost wariness each advancing step, do we safely pass over shaly rock, and around these cliffs, daring not for one brief moment to look downward, lest, with weakened nerve, foot and hand lose their cunning grasp, and we go downward with our packs to such destination as we know not of. Here, then, we are at last upon the summit, with the Arcadian valley in the shadows far below, and the great clouds marching over the vast timber belts,— perched, pack and all, upon the topmost stone of the monument of rock, with the old mountain conquered at our feet.

It is a barren victory, for though we are ten thousand feet and more above the sea, and though the guide-books tell us of the strange emotions that we ought to cherish, and though other visitors riding here by some trail to us unknown have made the record that there is nowhere in the world view so beautiful and majestic, still it is not so wonderful as we had hoped, nor have we large usury of payment for the hardest day's work we have ever had in many years of mountain climbing.

The vision sweeps the circle of a hundred miles or more; great mountains, timber-mantled and snow-crowned, encircle us; the lower hills are draperied with forests woven with velvet softness; the pastures are green and lustrous, like the English lawns; the great lake lies like a jewel southward in the verdure; and yonder crest of color is the marvel-gorge lifting its banners above the Yellowstone, started on its journey of six thousand miles to the Gulf of Mexico.

But there are other mountains where peaks as sharp and beautiful as these are visible; and this foliage is not so rare as the vestiture of Mount Carter, seen from Tuckerman's Ravine; nor are these pastures green, like the Conway meadows from old Kearsarge; nor is the desolation of this summit, albeit its scars are yet flaming red all over us, so grimly savage as Chocorua's peak; while lake and gorge, unless our weariness has somewhat robbed the eye of seeing, are not from this high mount of vision the marvels that they seemed, when we stood before them and saw, with slight interval of space, the rare beauties which are their heritage. There is a weirdness here, for the solitude is absolute. These vapor columns that we see are not the smoke of farmers' cottages, but the steamings of the springs. The lake beyond has no keel to vex it; there is no trace of village, nor human soul, perhaps for miles beneath us; and this is a weird land of geysers, mineral mountains, and chasms that terrify the eye. This region eastward is the Hoodoo land, with forests of stone, agatized trees, strange monsters stone-imprisoned, — a goblin land, carved into majestic weirdness by elements working in the solitude for ages. There is tragic interest here; for over these hills Evarts, a tourist, wandered, lost for weeks, feeding upon roots and weeds, until at last, a skeleton, crazed with suffering, he was rescued,— the published tale of his long wanderings not excelled in vividness by any tale of adventure in the English tongue.

But the night comes on, and we must travel long before we reach a camping place. The descent is easy, our heavy packs but lightly felt. The peaks grow purple as we go down, and the sun attends us with the beacon fires it kindles on the peaks. Great drifts of snow are along the way, and for two hundred feet we slide downwards as we used to do in boyhood; and we slake our thirst from glacier pools, and over the hills, in the trail we now have found, downward dropping into the darker shadows, we push on for the timber where we shall make our camp.

The hills are in terrace-like descendings here, and, though we hasten on for miles, the elusive forests are beyond us still. It is growing dark, and there is no prospect of reaching shelter before dense darkness comes; our only hope is to go down a thousand feet to the creek below and make our camp, although upon the morrow we must make weary climb again backward to the trail. It takes some Christian grace to thus add, without complaining, a useless journey to our pilgrimage; and the way is rough, thick-set with pitfalls, with yawning holes that wrench the wearied muscles. The valley of the brook is reached, but it is a bog, with fallen timber and tangled thickets running into marsh; the water lying here in brackish pools, as though snakes and crawling vipers might be encamped among them. We have been ankle-deep not once but many times in the treacherous bog. We are parched with thirst, faint with weariness and hunger, and not yet can we tell that, even if we can find foothold between the alder bushes there, we shall find a running stream. We separate and search, fearing each step in the advancing darkness, lest we may be engulfed. But the stream is found, — cool, limpid, albeit its banks are but blackened peat; on the other side the ground is hard, rising toward the mountains; forty feet away we drop our packs and hasten to make our fire, that we may see what place we have for the sleeping of the night. Hardly a moment after the fire is crackling, made of grass and branches, and at once we start backward to the brook for water. But so has the darkness come, that we cannot find our way, and only by a torch from the fire do we reach the stream, over which we have come scarcely five minutes before.

A confession of self-humiliation is not a pleasant thing, and were we not an honest chronicler, we would fain let the darkness of our camp hide the sufferings of a memorable night. We are famished pilgrims; eight hours ago, we ate our unseasoned beans, and the toil of half a lifetime has happened since. And now here beside the bog, with only faint hope that the tangled grass is not the hiding-place of snakes, knowing not where we are, or what things are close beside us, we sit down to satisfy exhausted nature with a bean. The can-opener is gone, and with frail penknife must we open the solitary can of oysters that we have. We can only half warm the liquid, and then with pronged sticks we fish out the mollusks, drinking the liquid as the "loving-cup" is drained by passing from guest to guest, the sharp edges of the can cutting us, and the liquid, though most nourishing, having unpalatable flavor of verdigris, with little bits of solder held in only half solution. We fry the bacon, holding it against the coals upon a stick; but it sizzles itself away, it catches fire, the toasting-fork is involved in the conflagration, and there is left only a charred ember, so curled around the stick that we cannot in the eating easily decide where the stick begins and the bacon ends. We essay to make some tea, and in the emptied oyster-can, only half rinsed, we fear, we place half a handful of the conglomerate in our pocket, making a draught compared with which the hemlock draught of Socrates must have been as the very nectar of the gods. We have no heart to tell of the course that followed. The bean, though baked in Boston, is not a fruit that epicures might choose for a dessert, but we are not encamped in the vicinity of markets, and our larder now contains no other thing than these same beans.

Guided by such light as the camp-fire gives, we pile the wood high for the night and make promises of watchfulness; then wrapping blankets round, with the great deep blackness over us, and such movement in the air as sounds like the whisperings of ghosts, we close our eyes to such sleep as our weariness may woo. The fire burns brightly for a while, the dried grass catching and causing us not once but many times to rise and beat out the spreading flames; but the fire is fed only with the substanceless cottonwood, and long before the morning dies to ashes. The great white frost comes on, and when we wake, long after the sun is up, we find the crystal rime spread over us, and cease to wonder why it is that we have shivered through the night. The breakfast is severely plain. Another can of the detested beans is opened, and nature is again insulted, not satisfied.

We have never had repugnance to the ongoing of our life, and have no ambition now to add to the legendary interest of the Washburn trial by leaving our skeleton here to adorn a moral or garnish a tourist's tale. But now we refuse to again put the detested cans within our pack, and vow most solemnly that we will not eat another bean though we may die upon the journey, considering death a pleasant fate compared with such repast.

Upward, with heavy tugging at our packs, onward five miles or more, and we come to the great open pasture space, shaded with mammoth pines, where the trail divides to go down and round the cliff, upward to Tower Falls. The path is tortuous, but great basaltic cliffs of sulphur are in sight, just where Tower Creek joins the Yellowstone. The way now is beside the stream, over such bowlders as the great cliffs have dropped. But the stream is close beside us, fretting, fighting over rock and jutting point, battling its way onward to the sea. Great towers, shapely as cathedral spires, rise on either side, with slender fingers, like the minarets of a mosque, strangely colored, forming royal setting for the water, which, from two hundred feet above, falls into the boiling chasm. The surroundings are much like those of Minnehaha Falls, only here is greater majesty. It is a mile downward by the path, while if we can but climb the walls of the cañon, we shall find the path just there upon its crest.

We begin the climb of four hundred feet. The wall is perpendicular almost, but so scarred and broken that it seems not difficult to find holding place for hand and foot. We are soon convinced that it is a fool's folly, but our blood is up, and we have no temper for defeat by a little wall like this.

Starting together, we are soon separated, each working on by different lines; up and over rocks, clinging to roots of trees long dead, baffled by sheer ascent of smooth ledge and rock, retreating, finding new paths, going on a little to be again defeated, pushing up, confronting obstacles, balancing the conditions of safety in going up or back,— so for two hours, at least, we wrestle with the cliff; almost at the summit once, we must go back, making the descent with peril. So onward, with every muscle tense as steel and every faculty alert, the jagged bowlders waiting for us down there in the gulf, and the pleasant sky above beckoning, we climb with painful toil.

At last, when only the pasture is fifty feet above, we come to a projecting cliff; we must climb over this or retrace our steps, and retreat is now impossible. The problem is a study while clinging to the rocks; but standing upon utmost tip of foot, blindly groping on the surface of the rocky shelf, we find a dead root, and testing it with gradually increasing power, we hazard at last our life upon its strength. Swinging clear, with no other hold than this, we climb upward and so onward to the summit, to lie there, with torn garments and scarred hands, till slowly the weary muscles shall be rested and the excited nerves become calm again. The others have found like peril, and half through the tramping of the afternoon there is little said, by reason of remembrance of the danger we have braved, and only by utmost effort been delivered from.

Downward still four miles or more, leaving Jack Barronett's bridge above us, we come at four o'clock into Pleasant Valley, in sight of Yancy's cabin, the only sign of habitation we have seen for days. No palace ever had such royal look as this "shack" of logs at the foot of the six-mile hill. We find Yancy's hired man in charge, and the star-route mail-carrier to the miner's camp beyond, stopping for the night. We rest upon the bunk of skins while these men prepare repast. Was there ever such kingly feast as this! Steaks of antelope, and great fritters floating in black West India syrup, and potatoes just a little soggy, and bread, saleratus-hued; but, oh! so much better than the beans! Never before did we eat so long with no increasing sense of fulness. After ten minutes' service we are just as hungry as at the start, and we begin to fear, perhaps, that the old story of Munchausen's horse, who drank dry the river because cut off just behind his mouth, might be finding modern repetition in these three pilgrims seated here in Yancy's shack.

We have always boasted of our pedestrian powers, but when we see the hill beyond and the great pack we have to carry, and know that the blessed Toot must be met upon the morrow sixteen miles away, our pride of walking vanishes, and we are like the old French bishop who used to say of worldly comforts, "All, all is vanity except a carriage!" and so we vow that we will not walk, though we may have to give our kingdom for a horse.

Neither the carrier nor Yancy's man can leave the place for an entire day, nor spare the horses for us; but in the road outside a shaggy-bearded teamster with a load of ore offers to sell, for fair consideration, an extra horse he leads behind. We are ripe for desperate things, and as we pass our pack and see the mighty hill beyond, we are in good mood for any folly. But such a horse we never before put eyes upon. It is a compliment to say that it is lame; every leg is out of shape, corrugated with spavin, ringbone, and every fungus that fastens on a horse, with only one poor watery eye, and such demure abjectness as we have never seen in a horse's face before. The critical mood is not on us, for we are in sight of both pack and hill, while our resting has revealed the stiffness of our limbs. Did the horse have but one good leg, we would surely buy him; but there is nothing on which to fasten hope of help, and so we say, "Why, man alive, we don't think that horse can carry himself over that hill;" and the miner answers, "I know he can't, and that is why I want to sell him."

We charter for the hill, however, Yancy's horse for the packs, and mounted on the star-route beast, with the man to bring them back, we go on. Life seems worth living once again, and when two hours later we dismount, we are fully rested, one of our companions meantime finding, as he walks beside Yancy's man, who leads the pack-horse, that years before they had been students together in a university in the Empire State.

By Black Tail Creek, at eleven o'clock, we make our camp, sleeping by the roadside in the open air, and on the following day, by pleasant road over the grassy plateaus and lava beds of the creek, beside the superbly beautiful falls of the Gardiner River, in sight of mountains now familiar to us, we reach our journey's end at the Mammoth Hot Springs, the place of rendezvous, where we are to meet in an hour's time the outfit left by us three days ago. While we sit on the ground, with back against a workman's cabin, reading a week-old daily we have borrowed, the leaders of our wagon come in view; and albeit he is no Apollo, we make confession that we have never seen before a man so absolutely beautiful as that same Toot, who is to carry us out of wonderland.

Upon the morrow, which is the Sabbath, we are beyond the borders of the Park. At the doorway of our tent at Yankee Jim's our driver leaves us for a moment, wishing to go, he says, to morning mass. We hardly think he means it, for, as we pass the saloon soon after, from beside the bar within we hear the voice of Toot saying to a fellow-driver, "Let us shake for drinks!"

# OVER THE ROCKIES BY STAGE.

*Thus far into the bowels of the land
Have we marched on without impediment.*
                                    RICHARD III.

# CHAPTER V.

### OVER THE ROCKIES BY STAGE.

HELENA is simply the old-time Crab Town in a later stage of evolution.

In the summer of 1883 it is the eastern terminus of the Northern Pacific Railroad and the metropolis of Montana. It lies at the foot of the Rocky Mountains, on the first slopings of the fair Prickly Pear Valley. The washings of the hills have made this valley strangely fertile, and nowhere have we seen more thriving farms or larger crops than in the region around this thriving capital. The city is built upon the tailings of a mine, for the Last Chance Gulch is here, and from the territory now cut into city lots and household yards gold to the value of ten millions of dollars has been taken. There is no poetry about the tailings of an abandoned mine; rocks and gravel intermingle, and barrenness is supreme. In the outskirts of the town, the little houses placed in the midst of this colorless refuse are pitiful in their abject desolation; but where larger wealth has built its homes, the tiny cottages sit in little lawns of green, and patient fingers have civilized the stony soil into fruitfulness.

The city is typical of this Western life. Luxury and rudeness jostle each other; frontier barbarisms mingle with the latest fashions from "the States;" the cowboy and the drummer ("time's noblest offspring is the last") eat at the same table, and perchance sleep in the same bed, in the taverns of this overcrowded city; while the electric light looks down on the strangest panorama of crowding, hurrying life that we have seen.

The railway approaches completion, only a few miles away, and Helena is the terminus now of the Continental Road. There has been a new adjustment of prices. With the coming of the iron rails luxury has entered; there is a larger outlook, a larger life. Helena is the supply city of the richest mining region in the Territory, and capital is coming here to plant itself in the new ventures with which the air is full.

There is a strange life here, and the casual visitor cannot fail to catch the feverish enthusiasm everywhere felt. Only with difficulty do we find rooms. The hotel is pretentious in outward appearance, but having behind this, where the lodgings are, the rudeness of the pioneer days; the electric light shines down upon the hotel office, and in the open safe we see at least a score of revolvers, left for custody by the guests. The street is filled with a motley array of vehicles : road wagons fresh from Eastern factories; great mule teams from the mines; the trotters of the city sports; the slow-paced farmers' teams; loaded stages from the mountains are coming in; while on the sidewalk tenderfoot and tramp, miner and tradesman, cowboy, prospector, farmer, move up and down. At night the city is alive; the gambler's den is open, and the concert hall sends out the twang of its guitars and the rickety voices of its alluring songsters; the roulette-table has its little band of victims; while in the side streets and multitudinous alleys of the city one sees such interminglings of thrift and poverty, such restless, incessant feverish toil, as causes every nerve to thrill with sympathetic restlessness. There are public buildings of imposing magnitude, fine churches, and no slight evidences of wealth. The general aspect of the city, however, is that of unrest, the temporary halting-place of an encampment; and while the business streets have showy solidity, one has but to go to the rear to see that behind these ambitious fronts there is a conglomeration of sheds and shanties, the architecture being, as some one has said, "Queen Anne in front and Crazy Jane behind." But nowhere have we seen such stir and movement; even sight of such activity gives exhilaration. Here enterprise can find a work and capital a field, while in the fairer homes that are rising — the changing of the old desolation of the mining-camp into a luxurious city — we see the evidence of the ameliorating power that comes with contact with the outward world.

One hundred and thirty miles away, far beyond the Rocky Mountains, is Missoula, our destination, where we shall find the railway which shall bear us down the Pacific Slope. A single wheelman has possession of the street in the early morning when we come out to take the stage, — the fattest rider, we will wager, that can be found between the two seas, — riding up and down with perspiring face and tottering wheel, causing apprehension as he sways, lest, if the expected fall should come, through the blockaded street our heavy coach will fail to get us out of town.

A journey to the Pacific over an uncompleted road is a series of disenchantments. We had dreamed of the passage of the Rockies on the summit of a Concord coach, with prancing leaders and strange adventures. The actual coach is a mud-wagon, — never a thing of beauty, nor designed as a palace of art or luxury. The wheels are heavy, and inclined to heat upon the axles; the seats are made of plank, veneered with the slipperiest of leather; the windows are half a foot too low for any kind of seeing out, while the venerable ark is so low-studded that with every jolting of the road one plays at shuttlecock with roof and seat, with constant questionings as to which has greatest malignity of hardness.

We had tried by every specious flattery on the previous evening to secure a seat from the saffron-haired dude that kept the booking-office; but the places were engaged, and we had only the sorry choice of riding upon the seatless top, or staying over till the completion of the road in the early autumn. The stage comes up, and we inspect the instrument of our two days' torture. We have not to sit upon the untempered oaken top, for a dirty canvas is tightened over it with long strips, which, with the natural suction of the body, will help to hold us on, we hope. There is no hint of rail; but the corners are so rounded that in our slippings off we shall probably clear the wheels, which is something of a comfort. The inside seats are filled; the driver has two passengers who have waited over to share his seat; the baggage of the continent seems to be piled upon the rack; the mail-bags are tied beneath the foot-board; and just as we hasten to climb up to select the slat on which we shall impale ourselves, we are told to wait till the baggage takes precedence. A zinc-covered trunk is made the background of the deck scenery, the rounded top, with half-driven nails protruding, and little scraps of metal reaching out their ragged edges, furnishing bumping place for our untutored spines. Bags of oats are then laid down lengthwise of the deck, the vacant place towards the driver being filled, at least a foot too high, with sundry satchels for our feet; the whole mass tied on with a wiry kind of hempen rope, which we may cling to if only we can get our fingers between it and the unyielding oats.

This is hardly the ideal we have dreamed of in our Eastern home. But we take our place with six other martyrs on the oats, braiding ourselves together as we can, — cowboy, miner, hostler, tourist, tramp, and parson, — not over sure that united we shall stand, but very certain that divided we shall fall.

The horses much need the oats that we can spare; the prancing element is wanting, but they are faithful, and deserve the pity that age commands. It is the last month of the old stage dynasty that once ruled from St. Paul to the Pacific, and these are the relics of a lost empire. We are the last victims of a dying tyrant.

The champion swearers of the world may be selected, and we will put the Montana stage-drivers against them, man for man, giving any odds that may be asked. They swear for very love of it, — at their horses, at each other, at marks along the road; they swear into the air, they soliloquize in oaths, with the smallest gamut, too, of curses; a brainless repetition of profane idiocies, that keeps one questioning his conscience whether or not it would be really murder to push the fellows off beneath the wheels.

To add to the felicity of our high perchings here, the brindle-bearded fellow that sits upon the box was "held up" on his trip the day before; his eighteen passengers getting out and yielding up, under the gentle persuasions of a brace of pistols, such little souvenirs as they carried with them. We are going over the same road with the same driver, who has a record of being the most-robbed driver on the line. There is little of the Pass of Thermopylæ spirit about our company; in polling the passengers, not one gives slightest intimation that he prefers staying back as a dead hero to going on as a live coward; and so thoroughly resigned are we to any arrangements planned by the "road-agents," that we verily believe a solitary man, with a stick, if only it looks like a gun, may capture the entire party.

The journey lies along pleasant gardens, through which the water flows from the flumes upon the hills; snug cottages, vine-embowered, are beside the waterways; along the road are noisy teamsters breaking camp for the long day's journey; and such pleasant odors come from grove and thicket as fill the world in the blessed morning of the day. The road soon rises in great upward reaches of the mountains. There is no sign of habitation now, except the little stations where we change the horses; but the forest grows dense. As the hills lift up, great peaks come out in line, and on the summits that we cross the vast range of mountains stretches far away, while into valleys, thick-woven with the braidings of the forest, we look down. Scene succeeds scene while we toil upward in this clear air; pleasant mountain-brooks are crossed, and were it not that now and then great peaks come in view, we might think that we are only tramping among the old familiar New England hills; for the same flowers are blooming here, and in deep vistas of the woods we see such beauty of fern and foliage as we have seen in other places far away.

The road is not all an ascending one; down great pitches of the hills, holding on as best we can, the heavy stage goes into sunlit valleys, with ruined mills and little fields musical with the mower's scythe. Here branches off the old road across the treacherous ford, — not longer used because of the tragedy enacted there a year ago, — and then comes the final climb to the Great Divide which separates the waters of the seas. The road is now a spiral to the clouds, passing by a cliff of iron, and up by winding terraces, until at last we reach the summit, and the streams go westward to the sea. We are on the Pacific Slope at last, and below us are fairer valleys than we have seen, green with the baptisms of living streams, with cattle-ranges beside the road, and great-eyed oxen looking at us as we hurry by.

Our forty-mile journey ends at Deer Lodge, and on the second day we move on towards Missoula. The deserted mine of Yamville is passed, with its old traditions of millions filched from the desolation of these yawning gulches; only the débris now is left, and over this the patient Chinaman is toiling, gathering up the shining fragments that are left. The town of Pioneer lies along the way, rich yet in gold, which these innumerable sluice-ways will separate from the sand. The water runs to waste to-day, for the miners have gone to the circus, twenty miles away. We are in the cattle-ranges once again, the long, rolling plains sloping upward into rounded hills, between which we can see great droves of cattle feeding.

At sunset we come to the famous Hell's Gate, — a winding way hewn out from the mountain's side; with mineral springs beside the road, and, fathoms down, the great noisy river with silent pools of blackness beside the shore. There are long level stretches beneath broad-branched trees, with such clean, needle-covered soil as old groves have; and then again the road winds up, looking across the chasm to sharp peaks, hewn into fantastic pinnacles, touched with such glory as the dying day can give.

The sun is fully set when, with the tally of sixty miles behind us as the journey of the day, we stop at Kramers for our tea. It had honorable record in the old days; but with the going of the stages the occupation of the inn failed, and we are set to sup upon the scraps left over from the feasts of other days. We have thirty miles yet before us, and we shall be fortunate if we reach our destination before one o'clock. The road has been heavy, and the dust and heat intolerable.

A construction train is just behind the house, for the railway coming from the West was built here a week ago. The train goes down in an hour's time to Missoula, and we will go over to the Chinese camp and wait, letting the stage go on, in hopes that we may find easier transit. We smuggle ourselves on board the caboose of the returning train. We have sailed in mid-ocean with less tossings than we now experience, for the road is unballasted as yet, and before us are the flat cars on which the rails are brought; so that the frequent stoppings of the train, for caution's sake, are like "the wreck of matter and the crush of worlds." There is a most unsavory smell within the car, for supplies for the laborers are brought in it daily up the road, while Irishmen and Chinamen, Greeks, Barbarians, Scythians, bond and free, are crowded here, going down the line. It adds slight comfort to the journey that the light goes out just when a spreading rail detains us for an hour. We have seldom seen so weird a night as this, here in the deep defiles, with the workmen's torches flaring at us in the darkness, and the noisy river murmuring we know not how far below.

A single lantern now burns within the car, changing with its flickering light the strange inmates into grotesque forms; the chattering of a dozen dialects long since has ceased, for the night is wearing on halfway to its close. We have found a little spot on the contractor's dining-table where we can sit, sandwiched between a Chinaman and a native of the Emerald Isle. They treat us kindly; for in the bouncings of the journey, so often as we are thrown upon them, they are never angered; and when tired nature seeks to "knit up the ravelled sleave of care," and in one undistinguished and indistinguishable mass we lie prostrate together on the table, we have rarely had — either because of weariness or the friendliness they bear us — more quiet bed-fellows.

So we finish the passage of the Rockies; not quite as we had dreamed in our plannings of the trip, but in easier fashion than if we had kept upon the stage, which, by reason of a fallen tree across the road, only finds the journey's end at daybreak.

We never learn what time it is when we come to the final stop. We only know that the international league upon the table goes to pieces at the first shake of the brakeman's hand, the Chinaman and the Irishman withdrawing from the triple alliance, leaving us as best we can to get awake and find shelter for the remaining hours of the night. The train stops short a little of its final halting-place, for the brakeman, to quicken us, cries out, "We only stop ten minutes here." Our scattered wits must be getting back, for we remember, as we scamper down, the old story of the desperado in the early days, who, being placed upon his mule, and told that he had just fifteen minutes in which to leave the country, quietly remarked, "Gents, if this mule don't balk, five will do."

# ON THE PACIFIC SLOPE.

7

*Where rolls the Oregon, and hears no sound,
Save its own dashings.*
                                        BRYANT.

## CHAPTER VI.

### ON THE PACIFIC SLOPE.

FROM the western gateway of the Rocky Mountains at Missoula to Portland, Oregon, is upwards of six hundred miles.

Leaving the mountains, the road passes soon into the Coriacan Defile, crossing the fearful span of the Marent Gulch over a trestle bridge eight hundred and sixty-six feet in length and two hundred and twenty-six feet in height. The road winds on along the faces of the hills, coming soon to the Jocko River, in whose pleasant valley for sixty miles the Flathead Indians have their reservation. These natives are peacefully inclined, having long ago yielded to the civilizing power of the Jesuits. River after river now is passed, the great ranges of the Bitter Root Mountains always in the west, until at last the splendid stream of Clarke's Fork flows beside the track, giving for miles every variety of pleasant scenes.

We have passed now into Idaho, having reached the most northern point of our journey. It is a narrow Territory, however, in this, its northern part, only sixty miles in width; but it has within it Lake Pend d'Oreille, one of the fairest lakes upon the continent. The track crosses the little estuary of the lake which runs up to meet the waters of Pack River, on a bridge a mile and a half in length, and then for nearly twenty miles winds along the lake's northern shore. The mountains rise grandly around the lake, thick with foliage of fir; bold islands are within the waters, showing no trace that ever a human foot disturbed their solitudes. The lake itself is beautiful, winding in and out among the hills, opening long vistas of pleasant river-like reaches of rippleless water. So for sixty miles the great lake hides for the coming people its rare surprises, rivalling our own Lake George in the beauty of the encircling hills and the serene loveliness of its pleasant waters. The shore is pebble-covered, like the beaches of the sea, strewn with sun-bleached timbers, and fragments of such rude boats as the Indians have made. Forest fires are raging on the mountains as we skirt the lake, patches of flame set on the faces of the cliffs making weird illumination, and sending out their clouds of smoke to drift above the waters of the lake.

The road winds southward now: the Spokane Valley is entered, and over the boundary line of Washington Territory we pass. The reservation of the Cœur d'Alêne Indians is close at hand. The natives here on the western coast are of milder temper than farther east, for they have yielded more readily to the civilizing influences of the Catholic missions, which have cared for them. A facetious writer gives as proof of the civilization of these natives the fact that "they sell their wheat for cash, and that the old chief, Sulteas, has a pair of well-matched horses for his carriage, and lets his money at two per cent a month."

The Snake and Columbia Rivers meet at Ainsworth, where we cross the river on a ferry. At Wallula Junction the Walla Walla River joins the Columbia, and our journey now will lie in the valley of this river. Yet not in the valley, for it has no real valley, as its waters are walled in by mighty mountains, and along the sides of these, on shelves and ledges, around out-jutting points, we shall go down towards the sea.

There is little fertility here, the desolation of the desert is around us; but there are massive sculpturings of rock and crag, and such mighty headlands as keep wonder all alert. The stone has crumbled into every fantastic form, while the great river below bears on its burden to the sea in mighty currents, hemmed in by crag and cliff. The Great Dalles of the Columbia are reached in the progress of our journey. Only yesterday the salmon season closed, and the town is alive with men. Fishermen, speculators, tourists throng the hotels, and as the great train noisily pushes through the town, crowds look upon it, waiting for transit down the line. The place has many curious sights, the new and old intermingling. Here in the old days the emigrant to Oregon halted his tired horses and embarked for easier progress on the river, and here too the new life of recent enterprise has found a place for its successful ventures.

Mount Hood, crowned with snows, raises up its kingly head eleven thousand feet, while the great river, compressed here in narrow channels, surges between its imprisoning walls. The scene is one of rare sublimity, for the shores furnish, with their black cliffs, fine setting for the angry waters, while over all the great mountain raises its majestic summit, looking down serenely on the wild passion of the river's flow.

If we could but call forth the strange adventures witnessed here, a narrative might be written before which romance would seem dull, for this has been the battle-field of the men who contended for the empire of the West. The Jesuit Fathers have sailed these waters, and while we glide along beside the river we can see upon the other shore the breaking up of the Indian encampments. The fishing season has closed, and from the settlements among the mountains the women have brought down the ponies to carry back the braves who have gathered here supplies for the coming winter. Long reaches of placid water follow, alternating with rapids; the great cascades of the Columbia are passed, the train noisily thundering beneath the cliffs, shooting through dark tunnels, to come out into new surprises of forest, cliff, mountain, and the enchanting river carrying its majestic waters half a thousand feet below our flying wheels. Down the cliffs, too, come great sprays of water, and deep defile and gorge lead backward in the hills; and there are traces of abandoned mines, and little cabins where the miners dwelt, with now and then a half-clothed savage, in defiance of the law, fishing upon the river's bank.

The track now diverges from the river, and, trailing through the forest for twenty miles, we come into the fair valley of the Willamette River; and here before us, across the river which floats the ships of every nation, is Portland, the metropolis of the Pacific Northwest. It has rare advantages of situation. Oregon with its vast resources pays its tribute here, and from these channels the great wheat-laden ships sail to every port. It has a population of nearly forty thousand, with streets of metropolitan breadth, great wholesale houses, street-cars, public buildings of generous proportions, an enterprising local press, and all the advantages that Eastern cities have.

We have reached now the western limit of our railway ride. Here we take steamer for San Francisco, and at midnight are on the "Queen of the Pacific," ready for our early morning voyage. An hour's sail brings us to the confluence of the Willamette with the Columbia, and on the larger river for eighty miles and more we sail to Astoria. The river is sombre in this early morning light, for the great hills on either side are clothed with forests; even the little islands are closely woven with the dense, dark foliage. Now, indeed, we realize the meaning of the "continuous woods where rolls the Oregon," for no villages cluster on the shore, nor pleasant farms relieve the sombreness of the unbroken forests. How grandly moves this mighty current; how wide it spreads in opening bays; how impressive are the solitudes of river, island, and the ever-present forests! Here is the old burial island which used to be the sepulchre of the dusky nation that lived and loved beside these waters; here are the places where battles have been fought, and these hills have given back other echoes than the shrill scream of our steamer's whistle!

The city of Astoria is curiously set upon piles, as though, with an unsettled empire behind it, there were need of thus filching from the sea a place for the city's site. The place was founded by the great fur company, and has had a strange and eventful history. It has grown but slowly, for until the building of the railway this wondrous region was but little visited. The salmon industry now is making strange activity, there being more than fifty canning establishments here. We visit them and all the wonders of the place. The town is still crude, and bears but slight evidence of wealth; but the great ships lie without in the harbor here, and in these crowded streets one feels the beginnings of the larger movement that is to change the old city into a place of thriving industries and commerce.

When the tide covers the bar to sufficient depth, we cast off our lines and leave the continent behind. The great headlands come in view, Cape Disappointment holding bravely up against the encroaching sea. The ship passes out of the river and is on the Pacific. For two days we sail upon its placid waters, no sail relieving the great wastes of water, nothing seen except the sea-gulls and the drifting weeds. The sun sinks with glory in the sea, and the balmy night reveals the stars above and the long starry way trailing behind our advancing keel. The air is fresh with the breezes that float above the sea, tempered, seemingly, with perfumes from invisible islands of fragrant woods; the forest fires are burning along the coast, and the vast ranges which would bear us company are hidden behind smoky veils. But the ship drifts on, and here before us are the shores of the golden State, and here, rising like sentinels guarding priceless treasures, are the double cliffs of the Golden Gate. It is not wonderful that the old voyagers passed up and down, never dreaming that this narrow gateway opened into an inland sea so fair as this beside which the great city has built itself. Were not these mountains veined with gold, this entrance-way would still hold worthily its royal name; for it is of surpassing grandeur, the rocks themselves bold, sea-scarred, holding up their defiant ramparts against the sea. The bay beyond cannot surely find — unless it be in Naples — any rival in the world; island-dotted, spreading out its blue waters like a sea, with pleasant shores set thick with towns, and on the heights the magic city of San Francisco, with its vast multitude of buildings, and over all the solitary cross of the burial-place, standing clearly outlined against the cloudless sky.

We can hardly realize that we have reached the wonder-city here upon the western borders of the continent; that California is before and the Pacific behind us. So, wondering at the strange life around us, we come down the gangway, feeling, as the throng of hackmen importune, that after all we are yet upon the earth, although so severely do they press us, we have grave doubts how long we may be permitted to tarry in the flesh.

# THE CITY OF THE GOLDEN GATE.

*There's something in a flying horse.*
PETER BELL.

# CHAPTER VII.

## THE CITY OF THE GOLDEN GATE.

ROME has the advantage of San Francisco on the score of age, but the newer beats the older city in the number of its hills. While "Jerusalem is a city that is compact together," this one sprawls from the Golden Gate half-way to the Sierras, — a kind of miscellaneous go-as-you-please sort of a place, that looks as if it had at first been built out of plumb, and by a series of earthquakes had been still farther kinked and twisted. The hills are real up-and-down sort of things, cut decidedly on the bias, crossway, sideway, endway, angleway, anyway, running up, looming up, any-way-to-get-up, made of sand which is so generally in a state of flux that a man hardly knows the next day on which street to look for his corner lot. The houses hold on to these side-hills by some indescribable suction, and it is said that the feet of the people, before the coming of the cable roads, so slanted by the climbings of the hills, that on level ground they had to walk upon their heels.

Shanty and villa intermingle, the houses of the rich and poor meet together; and ambitious architects are the makers of them all. The newer buildings are of imposing magnitude, of great solidity and grace; the homes of the millionnaires are palatial; but the general aspect of the place is that of a lack of architectural character, a city where every man owns a jig-saw, and is the architect of his own house if not of his own fortune.

An old South Jersey friend used to say, " Our land here is valueless, but our climate is worth a thousand dollars an acre." The average San Franciscan keeps discreet silence of the city's soil, but the climate is a constant theme for wonder, love, and praise. And yet the weather is as uncertain as the fulfilment of Vennor's prophecies. Summer is in winter, and cold weather comes in the hot months. About eleven o'clock in the morning the zephyrs begin to put the hills in circulation, and the entire unimproved estate of the city is up in air. The wind is a kind of marrow-searching affair, severely gritty, a trifle salt, and sure to make itself at home in the defective tissues. And yet these people with chattering lips will chant the praises of the balmy air, while the zephyrs make havoc in the streets, and there are fires in half the city grates.

We have told the truth, but not the whole truth, about this sandy soil. There is some latent power in these grains of sand which the California water finds, for wherever the magic water touches it the desolation changes to luxuriance. The city in many of its parts is a garden; tiny yards are like little bits stolen out of Eden, with velvet lawns kept green with daily waterings, and clambering vines covering porch and trellis. In the flower season the city must be like an Oriental fair, for here are fuchsia bushes like lilac trees, and great tangle braids of vines that must take on bewitching beauty when the flowers come.

We can believe the wonders that they tell us of, for in the great park we visit we see some of the marvels born from the marriage of this strange soil and the miracle-working water hidden in the hills; and even now, when the year wears its russet livery, we get hints in the belated blossoms of what the city must be,

"When spring unlocks the flowers to paint the laughing soil."

This is the way we see the city. In the Nevada Stables there is a horse, the fairest, rarest horse man ever sat upon. Our good fairy tells us where to find him, and he knows that we are coming, for he dances with joy to see us; and how glad he is all through the day that we have come to ride him! The genial Willis used to say that "there is nothing so good for the inside of a man as the outside of a horse;" and so do the Arabs have love for it, that they have an immemorial proverb, that "he who forgets the beauty of a horse for the beauty of a woman will never prosper." But there are horses and horses, and who can tell, by looking, the fashion of a horse. Even so wise a man as Sforza used to say, that "should one desire to take a wife, to buy a horse, to get a melon, the wise man will recommend himself to Providence, and draw his bonnet over his eyes."

But we know by that instinct that creatures sometimes have that both horse and rider have met one of the epochs in their lives, and the great splendid animal is so royally glad that we have come that he is impatient to bear us over the hills and far away in such an exultant race as we have never had in all our life before.

Oh, but it is a wondrous seat that we have found, — a very battery of electric force! We can feel beneath us the dancing of every nerve, and how airily this matchless creature bears us, as though he carries Cæsar and all his fortunes. We wear our honors meekly as he bears us through the crowded streets; we have just a touch of hope that those who watch us are giving not all their admiration to the horse; although so do we love it that we cannot be envious if we would, and secretly we know that we are not half so superb an animal as this that carries us.

But here is Nobb Hill, half a thousand feet above us; and how can this fellow bear us up this semi-precipice of plank? Ah, we little know him! We loosen our reins just the tiniest bit; and away, up and on, he springs, as though life had no joy so great as climbing to the clouds. We have come far to see these palaces of the bonanza kings, and really we must insist, now that we are here, on looking for a moment; for how can we tell now that we may not some time be millionnaires ourselves? — and it will be handy then to know what things to do. So, despite the protest of our horse, — though the feet dance, and the curb is flecked with foam, — we spy out the wonders of the palaces. They are vastly large; a very efflorescence of tower, turret, balcony, and portico, an epidemic of ornament, as though the jig-saw, being a plebeian fellow, had a kind of communistic hatred for the millionnaires, and had wreaked wild vengeance on their dwellings. We dare not say how much these pretentious buildings cost, knowing that we shall surely miss half the figures; we are certain, anyway, that the wall around the terrace on which this one rests cost a quarter of a million, and, as the humorist said of his frog, we could n't see any points about that wall any more than any other wall.

We begin to grow suspicious that in other days our horse has carried some hoodlum rider to the Sand-lot meetings; for where can we get, other than from him, the strange, protesting feeling that these dwellers here should have such palaces, when there is such poverty just below the hill? It does not seem quite fair that there should be such inequality; and as we look across the bay to where the prison is, and think of the convicts there busily working for the State, and then at these palaces. of the monopolists, we confess that we have a kind of hoodlum feeling as we listen without protest to this old saw that our horse repeats to us:—

> "The law locks up the man or woman
> Who steals the goose from off the common,
> But lets the greater villain loose
> Who steals the common from the goose."

Of course we will not countenance any such heresy, and we tell him to go on and mind his business; but as we go along we secretly think there is good "horse-sense" in what the fellow says.

Far off on the hills, set against the sky, stands on the summit of Lone Mountain a wooden cross. Far out at sea we saw this thing towering weirdly, like a second Calvary, above the city of a hundred hills; and now we will go upward to where the cross, in its place of graves, keeps its eternal vigil above the ambition, the shame, and virtue of the city. Down, up, over the hills, by pleasant homes, touching the rude fringes of the town, we come up to the city of the dead. Close beside it is Laurel Hill, beautiful with ivy, with no sign in outward glory of shrub and tree that there are graves beneath these scarlet and purple flowers. We can read here the story of yonder city's life. The pioneers were buried beneath these wooden slabs. How rudely they are carved! The weather has almost stained out the little record of their lives. This is the end, then, of the adventurous lives of the bold men who came over the plains and by the highway of the sea to plant here a new empire! How familiar are the names on these old moss-grown stones, — Providence, Newburyport, Boston, New London, Salem, Gloucester, New Bedford! All of these we read as the birthplaces of those who once were clothed in the dust mouldering beneath; and our journey through these silent cities, whose dwellers never move, tells us many things of the old life of this strange city of the Golden Gate. But here we are far above the city.

San Francisco is upon a tongue of land running up to the mountains, between the bay and the sea. On the seaward side the hills as yet are but sandy dunes, bearing only such faint trace of softer life as comes from little patches of wiry grass. But here below is the city. Its squalor is hidden from this height, and one cannot tell now that there are any shadows of poverty and ugliness to temper the brightness of the place, sleeping in its magic loveliness below. But our eyes will not linger long on any city, when beyond there is such a bay as this. Why is it that they never told us that Naples almost had a rival here? True, this is a State that has within its borders

> "Awful Shasta's icy shrine;"

it is the land

> "Where a wind ever soft from the blue heaven blows,
> And the groves are of laurel, and myrtle, and rose."

In its great forests

> "Aged trees cathedral walks compose,"

while

> "Afar the bright Sierras lie,
> A swaying line of snowy white."

But even such opulence cannot afford to leave out of its catalogue of beauties so fair a thing as the bay of the Golden Gate. How vast it is, running from the sea far into the valleys of the mountains! A thousand navies here can ride at anchor; it is an inland sea, fair with islands, set round with hills; with white towns nestling on its beaches, and great rivers coming down like azure streams to join an azure sea.

These hills beyond are wonderful for one who has the inner sense to see the colors that even a treeless soil takes from the sun. They are such heights as old Spain has; and, unless the deceptive air is cheating us, there are winding roads going upward in curious spirals to the sunny summits. And if we will only shut our eyes a little and let busy fancy do the seeing, there are quaint cities there with walls and gates; and underneath, rude fishing-towns, quaint with cabins huddling by the cliffs, and old fishers' boats spread over with nets drying beside the beach.

There are pleasant towns upon the other side: Alameda, Saucelito, San Quentin, San Rafael, Vallejo, Oakland, with its great pier running out a mile or more, the fair Nappa valley, and beyond all the great peaks of the ever present Coast Range.

How fair the city is upon this cloudless day! Its spires and domes are not so lofty as many other places we have seen, but this is a city builded

> "Like Aladdin's tower,—
> Begun and finished in an hour."

Our own short life more than spans its history, and lo! here float ships from every land, here are the smoke of forges; it is a city of factories and shops, a hive of industry, rich with art, glorious with achievement, bright with promise!

Westward now to the sea we go, great wastes of sand around us, with now and then a cottage embowered in vine and foliage, and over on the hills the great white fence enclosing the vast area of another city of the dead.

But this grand fellow beneath us has a native's pride in this fair city, and whispers that he has more in store for us; he has caught, too, the briny smell of the Pacific, and if we will only please let up a little on the lower reins that hold the curb he will not say a word about the others, but will become the winged Pegasus bearing us to the sea. We try to chide and tell him more than once that we are known at home as soberly inclined, and ask him what would Mrs. Grundy say if she saw such mad John Gilpin racings out here across the continent, so really it will never do; and so we "kinder" keep him down, though because, perhaps, we are not over strong, our muscles would fail a little on the straight roads beyond the houses, while a thousand times we say, "Was there ever such a horse?" And there never was. We are at the Cliff House now, and our good horse whispers to us, "You just go round and see the seals, and I will wait here underneath the sheds and bolster up my breath to show you what I can do on the park road home."

So we stand on the balcony of the hotel and look out on the great rocks, and the uncouth seals, and the innumerable sea-gulls; the great ship with every sail set, bound for the portals of the Golden Gate; the great illimitable sea, and somewhere out in the west the King of the Cannibal Islands, of whom we used to think in boyhood much oftener than now. The rocks here are broken into most fantastic form, massed together in splendid piles, black like ebony, and draperied with black sea-weed floating with the surging of the tides. The surf-men are dragging up the life-boat from the beach, for this quiet sea has its angry moods; and beside the rocks a pleasant road winds downward to the sand, and upward to the park and onward to the city, miles away.

A sea-horse must have been the sire of this fellow that carries us, for the sea breezes have seemed to put a thousand fires within his veins. Our remonstrances are vain, and the sign-boards of the park, threatening every kind of fine for intemperate speed, are without avail. What can we do, anyway, now that we are on, but keep on, if we can, and go with him to the city prison, to bail him out, if they will thus suffer atonement for the breaking of the city ordinances.

Men look at us and wonder; fat dowagers drive under the shelter of the hills to give us all the road; the policemen hide in the bushes, that they may not see a crime they cannot punish; while we go on towards the city with lightning speed, anxious of course to go with dignified sobriety; but we can't. By the awful monstrosity of the new City Hall, an architectural nightmare in poor brick; by the vast Catholic College; on to South Francisco; along the water front; down the outside and up the centre, in the old country-dance fashion,— so we see San Francisco. If we should give the names and number of the buildings, its population, history, peculiarities, we should doubtless filch from the guide-books the essential facts; and we have no heart to take from our readers what rare pleasure there may be in stealing from first sources.

The Chinese Quarter, of course, must have a word of notice. Here is a segment of a Chinese city. The stores are veritable China-shops, — tiny, decorated with all sorts of fantastic tea-chesty, fire-crackery kind of ornaments, looking like the pictured Chinese junks stranded in the San Francisco streets, or a multitude of transplanted pagodas. The stores are orderly; the little markets scrupulously neat, containing such little messes of curious vegetables as a picnic party of dolls might wish. The streets are filled with natives, — orderly, civil, not handsome, quiet, sober. We do penance for an hour at the Chinese theatre. The Chinese are not a histrionic people. The dramatic instinct is not strong. They are not, if our observation serves, "children of song." We should not select a boiler-shop if we needed the solace of music; we should prefer it, however, to a Chinese theatre. The tin-pan serenade of a bridal couple in a country town is like a symphony compared with the music of a Chinese orchestra; and we are confident that nowhere on the earth, or in the sea, or in the waters under the sea, is there such "confusion worse confounded" as at the Chinese Opera on one of the full-dress nights.

There is no curtain, no scenery, "no nothing" except noise. The orchestra is on the back part of the stage, pounding away for dear life: cymbals, drums, fiddles with one string, and that the squeak one, banjo-looking instruments of torture, a miscellaneous lot of articles by courtesy called musical, in the hands of a lot of able-bodied laundrymen, every one of whom is contributing to the general agony. The men smoke, have their hats on, stop to chat, light their cigarettes, exchange places, go out, and visit round generally, oblivious of the plot, — though there is no plot except to make all the noise they can. The supe walks around, waits till the actors get up, takes away the seats, leans against the walls, lights his cigarette, makes himself generally at home. Spectators go at will on the stage, and there is a kind of unconventional free-and-easy abandon to the performance, that would be exhilarating if our heads were not breaking with the pressure of the noise.

The actors are well dressed, though we cannot say that we are partial to the Chinese costume. Their speech is a kind of prolonged soliloquizing, uttered in a kind of falsetto key; it has this advantage, that a little of it goes a good way. We should have been satisfied if, like George Washington in the story, we had simply walked up and then walked down again; and while there are dissipations that we may repeat in the unfolding of our life, we are certain that our curiosity concerning Chinese dramatic art is satisfied, — in fact, more than satisfied.

San Francisco is a city of hotels. The Palace is, on the outside, an architectural patchwork of bay windows; the building within is set round a large open court covered with glass. The building cost seven millions, and is the largest in the world. Hotel life is in great vogue with the people here, and quite a fraction of the population can be found residing in the great public houses.

Among the pleasant and profitable things to do in the city is to visit the rooms of one of the great photographers. We select Taber's, the leader of the art on the Pacific Coast. Nowhere, unless it is in Venice, can there be such pictures painted by the sun; for nowhere has art attained greater perfection, and nowhere is there finer atmosphere than this. All the wonders of California are here, — a rare artistic instinct selecting just the one right spot for the picture, and then doing the mechanical work with the enthusiasm of an artist rather than the unthinking formalism of an artisan. The wonders we have seen are revived by these matchless pictures, and in these images of the new wonders yet awaiting us we feed anticipation.

The city, we think, is worthy of its location, and destined to achieve a splendid career. The people are outgrowing the evils peculiar to their early days.

Municipal wealth will come, and with it the adornments that wealth procures. These things we believe.

But we know that the horse which now rests from his labors in the Nevada Stables is the best horse on the continent; and had we been taxed, on our return from the exploration of the city, the sum of all our assets, we are certain, with the hero in the Irish play, who was threatened with a year's imprisonment for his stolen ride, we should have exclaimed with him, "Faith, and it was worth it!"

# THE APPROACH TO THE YOSEMITE.

*What thy soul holds dear, imagine it
To lie that way thou go'st.*
                    SHAKSPEARE.

# CHAPTER VIII.

### THE APPROACH TO THE YOSEMITE.

ONE hundred and fifty miles from San Francisco is Madera, and ninety miles from Madera is the Yosemite.

The railroad takes us to the former place, and forty-one horses take us to the valley. The coach is an open one upon the sides, slanting at the ends in chariot fashion, like the band-wagon of a circus, but covered with a light top of leather, and fairly hung on the old-time thorough-braces. The seats are like the old sittings in the Litchfield meeting-house as described by Mr. Beecher, having no softness except such as you carry to them, while the backs reach up their sharp edges just high enough to catch the weakest vertebra. However, not a word shall we say against this matchless ride. The equipment is superb; strong, fleet, well-groomed horses, an unequalled road, and such a driver as we never had before.

All day long, up hill, down hill, the steaming horses go, the long lash cracking over them, while, clinging to seat and iron rail in the wild excitement that rapid motion gives, we are carried on towards the happy valley.

We are fortunate in the passengers that are to be our companions for a week. An ex-member of the Legislature of the Empire State, whom we early call the Senator, full to the brim of old scraps of college songs, with no small wit at anecdote and story,—a fellow of infinite jest, mingled with such good sense as is seldom mixed in the composition of the ideal "good fellow;" the Secretary of the Grand Encampment of the Knights Templars, which meets during the coming week in San Francisco,—a college professor before he became a scribe, with pocket full of such decorations as the Sir Knights like to wear, and many curious experiences tucked away in his knightly head, which will naturally be shaken out in the ups and downs of the journey of the week; an engineer from Iowa, who in Mexico is making fame and fortune; a banker, who, though fresh from Ohio, neither holds nor desires an office; a dry-goods merchant, also from Ohio. There is also a venerable Texan judge, with a tall hat much the worse for wear,—a man full of legal lore, mingled with poetry, an enthusiast in all the wonders of the road, guarding as best he can the daughter that accompanies him, the only lady in this company of men. A neighbor of the judge's is journeying with him,—a most irrepressible young man, most unaccountably skilled in law for one whose head is crammed with all the songs ever sung upon the minstrel's stage; a most susceptible young man, who manages, by such shifty tricks as lawyers somehow learn, to always have the judge and the judge's daughter with him on the seat, quite content to have the father on the outer side, where the bulk of his attention must perforce be given to keep himself from falling out and his hat from falling off.

There are lots of places worse fitted than a four days' ride for entrapping the love of a confiding girl. There are so many attentions that a lone maiden hungers for on a stage journey, such marvellous opportunities for those endless questionings which belong to woman, so many places of danger where a strong arm is needed, that we do not wonder that the young lawyer gradually changes the young lady's aversion to regard, — this regard subsiding on the return trip into solicitude, and in the last stages of the journey into love.

The course of true love does not always go smoothly even on a stage. The old judge, in the intervals of guarding his hat, is wont to rouse himself and come to the protection of his daughter, when the artful lover, with matchless skill, winds the old man up on the oft-repeated stories, calling out, with such dissemblings as lovers have, the well-worn anecdotes, until, wearied with protracted speech, the old man forgets his wariness and turns his exhausted faculties to the task of guarding his much-battered hat from the perils of the roof. The dry-goods merchant, too, is a thorn in the lover's side. He is a dashing kind of fellow, and it is natural that the judge's daughter — being a woman, and therefore human — is not going, without a struggle, to become the affianced of this persistent lover. We do not think the merchant really loves her, — we half suspect he has a wife at home, — but he has that rare winning way, that gentle deference that comes perhaps from the business that he follows, but which at any rate is most beguiling to a woman. And then the passengers are pushing the fellow on; making little conspiracies in the stables where the horses change, putting together combinations to slip the merchant in the lawyer's place, urging on the not over-ardent rival on the ground of public duty, and then watching in a kind of careless fashion the legal Cæsar sulking in his tent, while on the seat behind the merchant whispers to the maiden such pleasant nonsense as men have always used since Adam wooed Eve in the groves of Eden.

So through the journey there is this little romance, — a gentle girl and a gallant youth, learning, by that tender tutelage that love knows how to use, to change each other from common beings into idols; the maiden urging on a lover's lagging steps by pleasant little coquetries, trying to cheat herself with little resistances, yet leading him on all the while. So the old, old story is repeated, until, when the journey ends, the young lady,

> "Tying her bonnet under her chin,
> Ties a young man's heart within."

The morning air is most delicious. We pass over barren fields into pleasant woods, with such frequent change of team as keeps the wheels, up hill and down, flying fast beneath us. We stop for dinner at Coarse Gold Gulch, where, not many years ago, a little band of miners took out in ten days ninety thousand dollars' worth of gold; but as they took it all, there is no occasion for us to stop beyond our dinner, and so we go on, through the pleasant defiles, beside noisy streams, with little touches of pastoral scenery close beside the road, and, as we wind over the summits, magnificent outlooks of vast range and pleasant valleys.

At Fresno Flats we find a pleasant village among the hills, and from this on the road is almost ideal in beauty. We have to pass yonder range of mountains; but so marvellously have these road-builders planned, that the grade is such an easy one that, beneath the cracking of the whip, the horses with gentle, easy trot carry us to the summit, miles away. In the greater wonders of the valley, visitors are apt to forget the beauty of the approach. The journey is long, the sun is hot here among the hills, and there is that expectancy that hinders admiration. But the road all the way is a delight, — winding over the hills in such graceful spirals, opening such vistas of enchantment as make the days, despite their weariness, memorable in the panorama of delights they give. More than once we are on great summits with lordly mountains looming up; little vales of Arcadian loveliness are entered, and just in the soft gloaming of the day we come into Fish Camp, a tiny valley set round with hills, with such soft, lawn-like turf and shapely trees as we thought could be found nowhere else upon the earth outside of the English parks. The long road, too, is set round with inimitable decorations. The fields are brilliant with flowers, — the old familiar daisies of the field, ferns with rare delicacy of spraying branch, shrub and bush as white as if frosted by the snow of a winter's day; and everywhere we see the wonderful manzanita, so curious in its bark of maroon velvet, so gnarled and twisted, besetting us behind and before, that we come at last to have most tender love for this peculiar shrub. So the day draws on, each hour unfolding richer beauties.

Now, farewell to fields and woods! We are in the California forests. The light is soft now, filtered down to us through branches a hundred feet above our heads. Truly did the old artists get from forest-trees hint of the Gothic church, and easily can we now believe that "the groves were God's first temples." How majestic are these mighty pines! clean of bark, broad-rooted, as they have need to be to carry to the clouds such massiveness of bulk; with great cones of green absorbing the sunlight a hundred feet above us on the pendent boughs. We are now in the region of the Mariposa Pines; just beyond, not many miles away, are the monsters that were growing here beneath the sierras before the white man's foot touched the shores of the New World; and these great columns that bear up the leafy arches of this doubly consecrated temple have stood here ages upon ages. Almost in silence we pass beside these monarchs of the woods, looking down into pleasant vistas paved with such rare mosaics as the sunlight gives when broken by the branches; while

"Filled is the air with a dreaming and magical light; and the landscape
Lies, as if new-created, in all the freshness of childhood."

Our driver will leave us at the end of the day's journey; but before he goes he will show us how cunning is his skill. The last stage of the drive is but four miles, on a down grade all the way, full of curves and twistings, — a mountain road running above deep ravines, with no intervening rail or fence. With foot set upon the brake, with such volley of speech and lash as these Jehus know how to give, the six fresh horses are started on their mad race; the coach sways, as it whirls around the narrow curves; straight down into the ravines we look, we dare not say how far; but on we rush like the wind, clinging to rail and seat, every muscle of the driver tense, and the horses wild with the excitement of the race. So we come to Clarke's, with sixty miles behind us as the journey of the day, and when we stand upon the platform we find that we have made the last four miles in a trifle less than seventeen minutes, which is not bad travelling for a public six-horse stage.

From Clarke's we make *détour* by special coach to the Big Trees. There are eight distinct groves of these giants in California. The Mariposa Pines are six miles or more from Clarke's, on an altitude as high as the summit of Mount Washington above the level of the sea. These trees are set apart by Government for perpetual preservation by the same grant that gave the Yosemite to the State of California. The trees number three hundred and sixty-five. They are stumpy in appearance, having rich brown, spongy bark; some standing alone, others in groups. The Grizzly Bear is the largest, having a single branch six feet in diameter. Twenty-two of us, with wide-extended arms, and hands joined together, are necessary to encircle it; and we have paused in our writing to measure the red ball of twine we carried with us and stretched around the tree. At the risk of being called a second Ananias, we give the measurement as eighty-six feet and eight inches; although, if any of sceptical tendencies doubt, we will not insist on the odd inches. We drive through one, Wawona, — it standing directly in the road, — and we are able to get coach and four horses all within the tree. These monsters are impressive things, vaster than we have dared to dream; but curious as it seems, they do not impress us with such sense of majesty as the more graceful pines that yesterday we passed, set in such beauty in the inimitable forest, with its lights and shadows.

Twenty-five miles now will bring us to the valley. We have left the lordly pines behind, but there are other wonders along the way. Steep climbings on mountain sides, new spirals winding up, great valleys dark as Erebus, and, nearer yet than we have seen, the vast sierras outlined against a cloudless sky. Should we turn back now, without the vision of the valley, we would be content; for all along the way there has been such shifting visions of delight as have made the journey easy, and now we are drawing near to the holy place; even now we are on the rim of the valley, and behind the veil of woods the wonder is concealed. By brook and under overhanging cliff, above the precipice and the dark foliage below, we come on and down; great peaks and domes spring into view; the wheelers circle round a ledge of rock; the motion ceases, for this is Inspiration Point, and there beneath us is Yosemite,— the fairest, loveliest valley that God has placed on the whole round earth.

# THE YOSEMITE.

*Where'er we tread, 't is haunted, holy ground.*
BYRON.

# CHAPTER IX.

### THE YOSEMITE.

WE shall not attempt the impossible task of describing the Yosemite. Had we ever dreamed that any pen could so fashion words as to give even an imperfect picture of this fair valley, the dream flees when from Inspiration Point we look down into the enchanted land.

We are on the rim of the valley, and all its loveliness lies half a mile of sheer descent below us. The valley itself is a picture of enchantment. Through all its tiny one-mile breadth there is an intermingling of forest and meadow, green fields and darker shade of shrub and tree; while through all its little six-mile length the gentle Merced flows in such enticing windings as never wayward water found before.

On the journey hither, we find that the summer's drought has parched the fields, and they are sere and brown, but wet with the baptisms of these mist-wreaths hanging like draperies from the sky; watered by the ever-flowing Merced, no gardens in fabled Arabian tales ever were clothed in robes so green.

The royal picture has more than royal settings, for it is framed in such majesty of mountain, dome, pinnacle, and peak as nowhere else surrounds so fair a spot on earth. And upon all this — the river winding amid sunlit meadows, the intermingling field and forest, the mighty cliffs lifting their Titanic masonry half a mile upward to the clouds — the eye rests from this mount of vision.

The descent to the valley reveals, from every one of its innumerable windings, a varying scene. El Capitan becomes appalling as we come near to the level on which its great bulk rests. The Cathedral Spires seem as though beneath them there must be the mighty arches of the temple which they crown, while from the summit of the valley the great Domes dispute empire of this kingdom with El Capitan, sitting through the ages here, with the Merced singing at its feet.

We will not profane this place by our petty measuring-rods, nor even attempt to give the catalogue of wonders; there is not in mere height or bulk grandeur or beauty, and it is mockery to prattle of names and dimensions when we are beneath the overshadowing of Omnipotence. Travellers have written that not at once does the Yosemite impress itself, — that one must wait in silence hours and days, until the spirit of the place weaves its magic fascinations around the soul. There is needed for us no such waitings for the spirit. The illimitable majesty of rock and cliff, the sense of immeasurable height, awe the soul, while the inimitable beauty of meadow, stream, and forest changes awe into an adoration that subdues speech, and fills the heart with such nameless rapture as music sometimes brings. Twice before have we felt that sudden hush of life, as though the inward spirit was awed to silence in the presence of Omnipotence: once, when we stood upon the platform in the forest and saw the wonder-gorge of the Yellowstone, with its majestic sweep and its transcendent colors; and again, when, at Canterbury, we stood in our first cathedral, and heard the music of the choir chanting the evening prayers.

We have no heart for any human fellowship in our communings with the spirit of Yosemite. The pestilent guides seek to force us to vulgar explorations, seeming, in their bargainings, like those who once sold doves within the precincts of the Temple; but we will not see the holy place profaned by a showman's babble, and so we let the tourists all drive off, while alone we sit and watch the meadows and the hills.

There is a time in a summer's day when the light is soft and tender, its glare is gone, its heat burned out, — a kind of Indian summer of the sun; and when this comes, we saunter out to meet the spirit of the place. We have open doors and windows for it, and with the first step upon the meadow it enters in and possesses us all through the blessed hours. We cross the Merced upon the bridge, and, turning down the valley, pass the gypsies' camp, and saunter towards El Capitan. No living thing in all the valley has dwelt among these cliffs so long as this river here, and we know that in all these years it must have learned where the largest beauty lies, and so we will follow it, rather than the highway that man has made. And the gentle Merced never betrays us in all the journey of the day. We follow all its windings; but so does it sing to us along the way, uncovering its shining pebbles, displaying with every artless ripple its grace of motion, that we have no heart to chide it, though it is leading us by tortuous windings into the darkness of the night.

We are drawing near El Capitan. How wonderful it is! Is there anywhere on earth a wall of stone with such Babel aspirings to touch the skies? Is it the light softening the stone, or such tempering of the granite as the waste of ages brings, that makes the massive rock wear a kind of tenderness as though it were the friend and not the enemy of man? Were it not that there is this hint of something that in living things we might call pity, this vast massiveness would repel rather than charm, as now it does. But the Merced whispers to us, "Look at me, I am the interpreter of El Capitan;" and there in its placid water we see the mountain, with every grace of drooping line, with every soft weather-stain and arabesque of fire, frost, and sun, canopied even in this magic mirror's face with the rare tapestries that the dying sun loves to weave.

This is the El Capitan that we will carry with us through the years, robbed by the Merced of not one cubit of its height, changed by no deception, bearing every scar and trace of sorrow left by the travail that gave it birth, but somehow glorified, as the Lorraine glass transforms the landscape; in some such fashion, as we have only clumsy wit to tell about, interpreted, as the master painter, giving to his picture all that nature gives, adds to it what nature lacks, — a transforming soul.

From the river, now let us go up and face the mountain. We will sit here and trace the mighty wall, inch by inch, four thousand feet to where it holds the old sky up. The eye climbs on and on! Will it never reach the summit? How broad it is, and what folly is it for this puny creature, sitting here upon these bowlders, which the mountain has hurled down and never missed, to be attempting with such poor things as human words to describe such wonder as El Capitan! We have seen in our journey along the Merced no human being; but now, just as we are in the forest, we meet two stalwart Indians, naked to the waist, of such hue as a burnished shield of bronze might have. So into the experiences of this rare summer's walk in Yosemite there enters this human element, which adds to our remaining journey such romance as busy fancy weaves, as we walk along in the gathering twilight. Oh, but it is rare sight to see the sun kiss good-night to these great peaks! The lesser ones are earliest touched, as children first are put to rest; and then one by one the higher peaks are kissed asleep, and the shadows of the valley have company in the mountain's shades. We are far away now from our shelter for the night; the Merced must be crossed before we can return, and there is yet no sign of bridge, and here in the forest already the darkness comes.

But what matters it, so long as nature is making, all for us alone, such transformation scenes. We have never seen before that night comes on with such glorious pomp, and we must hereafter notice, if in any other place, night comes to its sovereignty with such ostentation.

We are facing now the rare peaks upon the Merced's other bank; the vast bulk of El Capitan is behind us, but here are sharp spires, like the Aiguilles that sentinel Mont Blanc, springing up and up, as never temple spires towered, and yet carved in such symmetry as Strasburg's spire never had. While we stand in the darkness, awed by these, a faint light gilds the crest of Cathedral Rock, and soon, in its fair centre, there is set the crescent of the moon, poised with such faultless evenness as a cunning craftsman might use in setting jewel in the centre of a crown. We are in the midst of marvels, and shall not wonder, whatever happens; but while the light hovers there, we can but ask ourselves by what right of conquest the Crescent rather than the Cross is placed upon this temple not made with hands.

We have crossed the Merced now, and are homeward bound. There is no sign of light, nor any sound of wheel or human voice; but there are such rare odors as the woods distil beneath the gentle pressure of the darkness, and such tender whisperings as the pine-trees give when the day is dead. So we come homeward, silent and alone, — yet not alone, for the moon makes such little light that there is faintest shadow of human form, as though our spirit is disembodied and walks beside us, or as if the spirit of the valley is giving us guidance home, while through the meadows the gentle Merced winds along, cheering us in the darkness with the

"Beauty born of murmuring sound."

Right behind our chamber window all night long stands the old Indian Loya or Sentinel, a single shaft of rock, symmetrical as an Eyptian obelisk. Take the tape-line in your teeth and climb this pillar, and hang the line upon some rocky splinter on the summit of the spire, you shall measure off the tally of three thousand feet before your work is done. No other peaks save El Capitan divide supremacy of height with this eternal sentry, while in simple grace, in light and airy pose of station, it has no rival in this fair valley.

We steal off alone, to make, in the early morning, pilgrimage to see the sun paint the picture of the mountains in Mirror Lake. The landlord uses every art to dissuade us, fearing, with such solicitude as we can easily interpret, that we shall be unable, without serious fatigue, to make on foot the journey. But we have come across the continent to see this Yosemite in the way we best love; so in such delicious morning air and light as belong here we make our pilgrimage. Following up the Merced's trail to where it leaves us to climb into the mountain, across the fields by little pasture paths, in and out among the rocks, we come at last to the little lake.

The North and South Domes are above this mountain tarn, while towering over all, ten thousand feet above the level of the sea, is Cloud's Rest, the defiant Jove in this pantheon of the gods.

The way has narrowed now, and if we will make further exploration we must turn back and go eastward into the valley out of which the Merced comes. But we will not go till we see the fashion in which the sun leads his armies to the conquest of Yosemite. Above the eastern Dome, Tisayac, already there is the orange tinge which colors the liveries of the heralds that go before the king; the mountain's crest is gilded now, the gold changes to a flaming fire, and out of the fire comes the king to rule the day. Meantime on every peak the courtiers stand, crying "The king has come!" The sun's banners are hung everywhere on cliff and peak; the very woods are driving off the shadows that inhabit them; the Merced's ripples glisten like the silver scales of a knight's armor; the night has gone, and above Yosemite

"Jocund day
Stands tiptoe on the misty mountain-tops."

Shall we stand here and watch Tisayac, the goddess of the valley, taking her morning's peep into the mirror of her chamber? Even the goddesses may have the pleasant vanity that lesser beauty is dowered with; and modesty and prudence, too, tell us that man's clumsy vision had best not see how tenderly a beauty rising from her sleep first pays tribute to herself, nor learn the cunning arts by which even a goddess, before her mirror's face, fashions her beauty for the tribute of her worshippers.

Backward now a little way, then eastward into the cañon from which the Merced flows, we will go up to the sources of the river, far beyond the forests, toward the mighty peaks.

There are steep climbings in the way, and we put beneath us the four sure feet of one of the poor mules doomed by some irony of fate to endless service in Yosemite. He does not greet our coming as tired watchers hail the day, nor rejoice as a strong man to run a race; we know that he has been in hiding, that he might escape us,—for the guides tell us that these fellows even climb the trees to hide from their tormentors: but we try and tell him that we are not to blame for his misfortune, and that if he will safely carry us, keeping silence of all his troubles, we will give him such decent treatment as he never had; keeping silence, too, of our own misfortunes, and showing him how wondrously kind, even in Yosemite, we can be made by a fellow-feeling.

The Appian Way never had such wondrous things beside it as ornament the simplest mountain-path that trails through a forest to the clouds. We have seen on nameless New England hills such marvels of mossy rock, such entrancing lights and shades, such forest architecture and leafy decorations, as have changed weariness to delight, and transformed a pathway to an upland pasture into a highway to the chambers of the gods.

But all the wonders are not here beside the path: we are climbing into an amphitheatre set round with such sculpturings as Omnipotence carves when it would make a masterpiece. Liberty Cap, the Half

Dome, before; the mighty wall of Glacier Point behind; beyond, the fair valley; around, marvels of forest, cliff, and waterfall. It is all wonderful, indescribable; majestic strength married to majestic beauty.

We have come to the great wall of stone which makes a barrier to advance; and over this, six hundred feet, comes Nevada Falls, one of the grandest cataracts the world contains. The settings are of incomparable grandeur; for the Cap of Liberty towers over it, and the wall of stone, down which the torrent falls, is such a one as Titans might build to guard their citadels. The water comes over the crest with great, forceful might and volume; angered with interposing obstacles, it breaks into little petulancies, — bursting out in passion freaks, stormy froth and foam, but, changing speedily into pleasantness, it weaves itself into such magic lace-work as water never fashioned elsewhere in the world, while in very ecstasy of power it toys and plays with the falling water, tossing it as a magician's balls, and changing it by some rare necromancy into mist and vapor.

Downward into the valley a mile or more the water, having rested in the journeying, leaps again in Vernal Falls four hundred feet. It makes the spring, not only because there is no other pathway to the sea, but in sportiveness as well; for do we not see, when we come below, the rainbow-ring which the fairies hold for it to jump through, if it can? But so does the water forget the taunting of the fairies, and stop to braid its lace-work fashionings and weave its gossamers over all its journey down, that it misses the golden ring which the fairies hold, — unless, perhaps, they with naughtiness have turned the golden ring aside, that they might laugh at the discomfiture.

The ride homeward brings relief to the long tension of the day's admiring. We have left behind — ungallant fellows that we are! — the bedraggled women who kept us on the upward road, conscious of the miserableness of life. They were strangers to us; but this is no excuse for lack of service. They were not beauty incarnated; but women cannot all be fair, and we think the little remnant of the conscience that yet abides with us would have made us reasonably attentive, for duty's sake. But when upon a mountain path one is sandwiched between a dowager long gone forty, fat, too, though not fair, and a maiden not yet forty, though neither fat nor fair, and the shuttle of an endless prattle is flying back and forth beside our ears all through the weary climbings of the day; when, too, we are half the time dismounting to fix girt and rein, to pick up shawl and wrap; when in the endless gettings down we have to catch good armsful of perspiring beauty, and in the gettings up to lift with most muscular gallantry these fair creatures, with scream and ejaculation, smothering all the time a wicked swear behind a smiling face, — it is not wonderful when, by some good ordering of our fates, we chanced to be ahead on the downward road, that with whip and spur we should have fled like new St. Benedicts, leaving the ladies far behind, to wreak their prattle on the guide, who, being a bachelor of years, doubtless needed such grace as comes from woman, whom, the poet says,

"Nature made to temper man."

Away from the mountain, we are now on the valley road which goes beside the Merced homeward. There has been no chance upon the mountains for such exhilaration as rapid riding gives, and so now in mad racings we go down the valley, forgetting the decorum which belongs to men of age and soberness.

The more active of our party are with us now: the Reporter, mounted on a spiteful mule called Jesse James, most curiously ornamented with a tail half-shingled in double flounces; another, riding the mate, though not banged as the namesake of the bandit; the mule we ride is fashionable in color, being of the old-gold shade, but having the quintessence of all the laziness ever given to mules since the world was. We have not sounded yet the depths of his depravity; so when one of the youngsters of the party drops behind and mildly asks us to take the part of prompter in a little panorama planned, we readily assent, desiring in good faith to do our humble part.

The conspiracy is this. The Senator is making his first equestrian ride this day. He is of the long and Cassius kind of men, whose legs were somewhat overdone by Nature, leaving slight residue of matter with which to make his body. He is by no means disproportioned, except when mounted on a horse; and then it is simply honest candor to say that he does not look like a centaur, — animal and rider one, — as perhaps those of us mounted on the mules appear. He sits, or, perhaps to be more accurate, is folded, round a large brindle-shaded horse, not over-sanguine in his temperament, though one cannot always tell what latent traits may be developed even in a horse under provocation. Whenever this piebald brute essays to trot, the Senator drops the reins and clings to the saddle's pommel, beseeching us that we go slower, as becomes a senator who has never before been astride a horse. The young men suggest to us that they would get themselves on each side of the Senator, and we should come close behind, and then at a given signal we should start the cavalcade in such mad flight as whip and spur could give, each helping, as he could spare belaborings from his own horse, to urge on the Senator's steed, which, by reason of being the larger animal, and the rider's hands being occupied, would doubtless need such help as we could give.

We do not remember at this writing just the things we said to break up the conspiracy; we know that it struck us at the time that we had a most excellent place, as we rode behind, to see the celebration, and that, so far as whip and spur could help us, we would keep as near the festivities as might be possible.

With a mad "hurrah!" the young men start, delivering every alternate stroke upon the towering horse on which the Senator all unconscious sits. The maddest gallop now takes place; the Senator clinging with persistent grip to mane and saddle, the tormenting youths applying whip, and laughing in wildest glee at the tossings of the victim of their sport. But the old piebald is warming with the fires of other days; the boys have need of all their energies upon their own beasts, for the Senator is far ahead, riding in such mad speed as the old mare has not made for twenty years at least, while despite the endeavors of the boys, urged on, too, by the taunting derision of the Senator, the twin mules stagger on in the proverbial discomfort of a stern race.

We, at least, have easy conscience; not by one stroke do we urge on the assailed steed, for despite such thrashings as we never gave or took before, we cannot keep within gunshot of the flying crowd, finding only such consolation as comes from a conscience void of offence, and the elaboration of the hypothesis, that while the old-gold shade is in good form as a color, it is not favorable to high speed in mules.

We do not like to say a word against either a bridge or a mule that has safely carried us, but we do not think that we are treated quite with fairness. The other boys, dismounted, are on the piazza when we arrive. The entire company of the hotel are with them, too. We plan to ride to the platform and give our mule to the boy in waiting to take to the stable. But the mule has his own private plans. He is no stickler for forms, and has no preference for the boy over his present rider. He bolts for the stable by a short cut. Our own plan is to let him go, but the entire company derides us.

We then try to coax or drive him to the steps. But, no, though we stop him, so often as we pull he turns his long face round, laying his appealing nose upon us, while his feet beneath, without the divergence of a hair, keep right on toward the stable door. We manage, under the spur of the derision of the company, to even get him pointed toward the house; but the rascal is a double-actioned fellow, and is going backward in the direction of his crib. The strategy of a leader sometimes rises in emergency: we let him go, steering him as best we can, until at last we have backed him up against a huge tree, which holds him fast. We have stopped him; but this is not victory. The taunts come thick and fast from the hotel, when, elated by our partial triumph, we steer him off from the place where he is stranded, hoping now by some favoring tack to fetch the stoop. But the mule has the courage of his convictions, and steers straight for the stable door, and were it not that a friendly hostler catches him at the threshold, we should not now be living to tell the tale of our discomfiture.

We cannot describe all our hours in Yosemite. We have no space to tell of the rare beauty of the Bridal Veil, the Merced's meadows, the vast peaks, the thousand fascinations of the enchanted valley; and had we space, our words would only be a witness against us of the folly of an ambition that dares to describe what is indescribable.

We will go out of the valley by the way of Glacier Point, which is up these walls three thousand feet.

Oh, but it is a rare walk we have in the Indian summer of the day! Every peak and waterfall, the winding Merced in all its length, are here before us; and each terrace that we climb, and every point we round, and every little summit we surmount, is a place of revelation. So upward, five miles or more, we go on this blessed summer's day, coming to fairer loveliness with each advance, wondering how Nature can surpass this scene, and yet finding at the next turning of the road that even Nature can outdo herself. So we come to the very tabernacle of the Most High, —

> "Mounting to Paradise
> By the stairway of surprise."

Not once, but many times, do we stand that night on the dizzy height and look down into the valley, sweep the heavens with our vision, and see with what audacity the great peaks have almost finished the task of reaching heaven which the babel-builders left incomplete. We look eastward to the great cleft in the fairest mountains on the continent, where Nevada and Vernal Falls make the sources of the Merced's loveliness. We watch the sun go down; we see over the Sierras the sun rise to give the world another day, and through the night such glory as we never expect to see again upon the earth.

And now the hour of parting comes, and as guilty mothers who desert their children kiss them in their cradles and flee away, so while yet the darkness rests upon the valley we will whisper peace and farewell, and hasten from Yosemite.

# THE ORANGE-LAND OF CALIFORNIA.

*And I said, " If there's peace to be found in the world,
A heart that was humble might hope for it here."*
THOMAS MOORE.

# CHAPTER X.

## THE ORANGE-LAND OF CALIFORNIA.

### I.

#### PASSADENA.

IN the plannings of our trip, nothing held greater place than the sunny orange-groves of Southern California. Some one has said, "There is a wild man sleeping at the bottom of every drop of blood in human veins;" and we are certain of it, for we have strange love for vines and flowers, the tangles of untamed woods, and most devoutly hold that next to a little child a tree is the fairest thing God ever made.

There is no spot in Europe so beautiful as the plains of Lombardy, between the alabaster spires of the Cathedral of Milan and the Alps. Patient industry has softened the ledges into soil, and the fruits of every zone have changed the fields into a magician's gardens. The orange and lemon, great thickets of oleander with spikes of pink like flames of fire, the darker cypress, laurel, and myrtle, all are here, and the tourist walks among them with wondering apprehension lest the conjuror's spell will break and the fair vision pass away. The Alps brood over this scene, and above the twining vines of this delicious region there is the subtle tropic air which makes the days spent on the shores of Maggiore days of enchantment.

Southern California in many ways rivals this fair spot in Italy. The mountains are here as they are there; not lofty like the Alps, nor covered with eternal snows, but scarred with such traceries as old Time makes. There is lacking, too, the subtle charm of water, which, Goethe says, "is to the landscape what the eye is to the human face;" but there is here the same luxuriance of nature, the splendor of the same foliage, the same grace of color, the magic of the same sensuous, dreamy atmosphere. Nature is prodigal of her favors here, and it was not wonderful that under the shadow of the old Spanish missions there should have been distilled out of this perpetual sunshine a dreamy life, lacking the high endeavor nurtured in fields where Nature more niggardly guards her riches. It is a land almost of eternal summer, and here between the sea and the mountains is the place

> "Where Winter keeps watch and ward,
> With Summer asleep at its feet;
> Stands guard with a silver sword,
> Where the Junes and Decembers meet."

There is something, too, in these pleasant names of Los Angeles, Passadena, Sierra Madre, San Gabriel, akin to the fair names of Baveno, Pallanza, Fariolo;

and these orange-groves and vineyards, the ranches where the shepherd tending his flocks lazily watches for the far-off islands of the Pacific, the pleasant nooks where the bee-farmer lives among the flowers watching the gathering of the honey, seem not unlike the things of which Virgil sang in his old pastorals.

The city of Los Angeles has many curious things for one who will get beneath its outward New England bustle, and find the old flavor of its Spanish life. There are quaint buildings of the old Mission days, streets where the Spanish names, half-faded out, are still upon the battered adobe walls; and in these crowds which throng the sidewalks one sees the peculiar type of Mexican face, and the quaint dress of the Southern nation that once ruled here.

We have little love, however, for the cities that lie along the way. They differ in outward details, but the places of business have essentially the same life.

We have come to see the Orange Groves. We will take a span of horses in the lightest buggy we can find, that we may make long journey and catch the exhilaration that comes from rapid flight. There is rare charm about this morning air, and our gallant steeds are entering jubilantly into the glory of the journey, and we can almost feel — in the quivering of the lines and the exultant pride with which they bear us — that they know they will give us rare surprises before the stars come out.

The way is dreary at the first, for the dust is thick and the fields are parched, the watercourses everywhere are dry, and the cotton-woods that are sheltered in the little gulches are gray with dust, like olive-trees.

We rise to higher levels, and here before us are the wonders we have come to see. What has happened to the soil? It has changed from a desert to a garden! Orange, lemon, apricot, walnut trees, so lustrous in their rich greens, set in such long lines that one can look as through a vista into fairer fields beyond.

We have read somewhere that these long lines grow monotonously weary with continuance of seeing, and that the brown earth beneath robs, by contrast, the trees of loveliness; but we only see the trees themselves, smooth of trunk like young apple-trees in a New England orchard,—a little short, perhaps, for perfect symmetry, but wondrously fair, with their deep, rich foliage starred with golden fruit.

The mountains always are in sight; the road winds upward to pleasant slopes, from which the great valley running to the sea is seen; in the zanjas, or irrigating ditches, the water flashes, as though from the mountains a stream of diamonds floated down to adorn the orange-trees; the tiny cottage of the small farmer, the semi-palatial residence of the rich, are set backward from the road in the midst of flowers and clambering vines; the workmen are making little trenches beneath the trees for to-morrow's watering, and beside the road hedges grow, and flowering plants, in the full luxuriance that comes from the magic water flowing at their feet. This is Passadena, the paradise of fruit and flowers.

The Sierra Madre Mountains through the ages have sent down their soil to make these fields, and from the mountains comes the water that has changed this desert to such beauty. These orange-groves, the flowers that girdle these little homes, these vineyards bending now with the coming vintage, all have come from "the rivers which run among the hills," making Passadena, if only it had the old associations of other lands, hardly less fair than the towns of Northern Italy.

But our pleasant musings here beside the orange-trees are interrupted. The road is hard as steel, and so smoothly roll our wheels along, and there is such exhilaration in the air, that when our bay and sorrel at the pole stretch out a little, just to try their paces on the Passadena boulevard, we have no sort of heart to restrain their racings, but let them go in mad John Gilpin flight, confident that somehow we can ride as fast as they can carry us.

We have just finished a little spurt like this, and have come down to such steady, even-goings as is the normal action of a livery team, when, without hint of warning, the horses loom above us, the carriage is climbing over and collapsing round us, while the nigh front wheel which has journeyed with us all the way is running off alone into the ditch to escape the catastrophe. We are tumbled up against the carriage side; our companion rests serenely over us; we cannot quite gather the reins to hold the horses; and there is a kind of dancing, ominous motion in the sorrel's heels which does not please us, as on three wheels, with a tottering, swaying buggy, we try to extricate ourselves.

The last spurt did the business for us; for the horses have not yet got wind enough to drag these frightened Yankees through the rest of Passadena in a three-wheeled buggy, and while the horses are hesitating as to whether it will pay to kick, in a kind of miscellaneous rolling out we disembark and place ourselves at their other end, where greater safety lies.

There is nothing flattering to the pride of an ambitious tourist in being away from home with a pair of strange horses, and this kind of a tricycle carriage. Even the orange-trees fail to fascinate. We fish the stray wheel out of the irrigating ditch to find that the nut which holds it on is placed at the back of the wheel in place of the front of the hub, and only the blacksmith's wrench and file, a mile away, can serve us. So out into the Passadena dust we get, our companion driving as the ploughboys do within the fields, and — shall we say it? — we jogging on beside the treacherous wheel, punching it on with our guide-book whenever it shows signs of again "taking water."

We are now in sight of the little village, but have no heart to thus enter it; and so by way of experiment we get into the carriage, hoping, when the wheel shows signs of coming off, we can stop, and from within pull or from without punch it on.

So we come into Passadena, — not proudly as we had hoped, but with humility of spirit; and while we cannot tell one word about the houses that are in the village, we can tell the number of the spokes, the color of the felloes, the full particulars of all the scenery of that detested wheel. The sooty fellow who serves us at the shop is laconic in his speech, for when we ask him, as we start, what we have need to do, he simply answers: "Drive slow, watch your wheel, and go back and give the owner Hades,"— though he uses a different translation of the closing word.

The Sierra Madre Villa is just under the shadow of the mountains, far up on the slope, with the great valley in all its loveliness spread like a picture at our feet.

The house is owned by an artist, but is kept as a hotel; it is beautiful in architecture, and surpassingly fortunate in its location. The view is matchless, —

mountain and field, orchard and vineyard, intermingling with far-off ranges, and fair trees shading the piazza where we sit. The honeysuckle covers the trellis of the house; a lawn kept green with flowing fountains is set round with flowering shrubs; and here is fruit of every kind: the golden orange, the lighter-hued lemon, the purple fig, apricots, nectarines, peaches, and such great clusters as the spies of Israel brought back from Eshcol.

We take long siesta here, yielding to the seductive witcheries of this fair spot, — plucking golden fruit from greenest branch, robbing vines of delicious clusters, eating the rich, ripe figs from overhanging boughs, forgetting that even in this land, "in which it seems always afternoon," the sun will set and the darkness come.

On the return ride we visit some of the great vineyards of the San Gabriel valley, passing on the way thither from the mountain through pleasant avenues lined with the acacia, pepper, and purple eucalyptus trees. The Sunny Slope estate lies along the way, and we turn our horses into the roads which wind over the twenty-three-thousand-acre farm of Mr. Rose, its owner. A company of Chinese laborers are busily preparing ditches for irrigation, working zealously with no overseer, as none is needed to make them faithful in their work. Here are sixteen thousand orange-trees, set in almost interminable lines, while eleven thousand vines helped to produce last year the grapes from which six thousand gallons of wine were made in the great distillery upon the place.

The proprietor's son is glad to devote himself to us, taking us into every part of the vast buildings, showing us all the processes of distillation, and giving us pleasant narrative of the gradual growth of this great estate. His father was a teamster on the plains; he had found but poor success in all his ventures, until he came here and planted his vines in the fields of this fair San Gabriel valley. New acres were added, and the little vineyard grew: a rude wine-press was set up, and wine was made; and so each year had seen an enlargement of the estate, until now it is the largest, richest one in all the valley.

We have been much interested, in our travels, in getting the opinions of the people regarding the value of Chinese labor. The Chinaman by no means is regarded with disfavor by all classes. Men of large business interests have spoken with enthusiasm of his work, saying that California is large debtor to him; that without his labor its industries would be undeveloped, and to banish him now would be to demoralize and destroy half the business of the State. Seeing that Chinese labor is largely employed upon this estate, we ask our guide as to its efficiency. The intelligent man answers in enthusiastic praise of his workmen, " Without them we should be helpless. They are industrious, tireless, painstaking; they never shirk; they need no taskmasters; they have intelligent interest in the employer's welfare; they are careful in the use of tools, destroy little, and are always willing, reliable, patient." Asking him if they were cleanly in their living, he replies, "You shall see." And so he takes us to the house where fifty live, showing us the places where they eat and sleep. Long rows of bunks are around the building, with cleanest matting of straw for mattresses; the walls scrupulously clean; the floor is scrubbed to whiteness; the kitchen is savory and sweet; we lift the covers of the kettles upon the stove, inspect the pantries, and examine the food, to find everywhere surprising order and cleanliness; while the stolid cook follows us with his half-opened eyes, wondering what business these strange Melican men can have in thus inspecting the domestic economy of the Chinaman's home.

At sunset we come to the old Mission Church of San Gabriel. It is of rude architecture, made of the rough adobe. Within and without it is poor, unsightly, poverty-stricken, having no other charm than that of age; and only with reluctance do we put the fee, fixed by the thrifty priest, into the hands of the withered hag who looks as though she has come up out of the old graveyard here to let us in, and when she has fastened the weather-beaten door behind us she will crawl back again into her grave.

The ride homeward to the city in the early evening is full of beauty. The mountains hold the light, while yet here in the valley we are journeying in shadow. The magic water does not reach us here, and the fair orange-groves are left behind; but there is witchery even in these bare fields of San Gabriel, now that the night is coming over them. Our good steeds snuff the stable now and catch already the glimmer of the city's lights; and winding round the pleasant hills, sweeping with clattering hoof over the great plains, with steaming flanks, they bring us home, so filled with sweet remembrance of the day that we have not the heart to give the horses' owner the thing advised by the sooty smith who fixed the wheel in Passadena.

---

## II.

### RIVERSIDE.

As yet we know nothing of Riverside. Passadena, we have found, is divinely beautiful. This is a girl's adjective, but we stand by it.

The people there are of gentle blood and culture, and when we asked them, with an honest wonder that seemed to please them, "Is there anywhere in California another spot so fair as this?" they answered us, "No, there is nothing like Passadena, unless perhaps Riverside may be compared to it." And so whenever we asked the question, so often we heard the name of Riverside mentioned by these gently jealous rivals.

We have a friend at Riverside who has sent us an invitation to visit him, and so we will go southward sixty miles, and at Colton leave the road to visit this fair colony. We find our friend, and are led captive to "Cosey Nook Cottage," to find royal hospitality. The house is the tiniest kind of a home; its thresholds even with the ground, with a piazza around its little front and side, shaded with the graceful semi-tropic pepper-trees, wreathed round with vines which clamber over its front and around its sides. The little irrigating channel is just beyond the sidewalk, and in a day or two, a swift, clear stream will flow by all the trees, and make many rivers around the roots of the ten thousand flowers of this fair village.

The house within is a thing of wonder, — rooms so tiny we wonder how any one can turn around without going out-doors, and yet somehow so elastic that once within there is abundant space; ceilings so cosily low that one feels at once that here is home indeed; and such curious halls and rooms and passage-ways outward to the orange-trees, such vistas, too, through the dark chamber of the long grapery stretching far away into the sunlight, that there seems to be an unreality about it all. There are no busy little fingers to meddle with the various devices of a woman's ingenious hands; upon wall and mantel everywhere there is woman's taste and genius beautifying the home; and really we would like to put our shawl-strap around the cottage, and carry house, inmates, and clambering vines away with us, setting them down in one corner of our city lot at home, that we might find refreshment for our weary eyes, as through the autumn days we do our work at our study windows. We have not yet made ourselves accustomed to the littleness; and when to-day we all went out we could not refrain from charging our host that he carefully close the doors that the dolls might not get out.

There are orange-trees around it, too, and a little vineyard, and from the pleasant hammock made of barrel staves, on which we took yesterday's siesta, we looked straight up into the broad-leaved fig-tree, and had but to reach upward to pluck the fresh, ripe, luscious figs. And then did ever mortal have such luxuries: walnuts, peaches, fruits of every kind, grapes of numberless varieties, and roses of such delicate hue and odor, — all within the little orchard of this tiny house?

Thirteen years ago the site of Riverside was part of the vast desert-like plains lying here in the sun between the mountains. The town is situated between the Sierra Madre and the low Coast Range mountains. It is in what is known as the Upper Santa Ana valley; that is, on land drained by that river, although not really valley-land proper, the quality of the land being rather that of the mesas, a chocolate-colored loam, rich in oxide of iron, and formed from decayed vegetable matter and the granite wash from the mountains, — a soil peculiarly adapted to fruit culture. The mountain views are superb. Cucamonga, Grayback, San Bernardino, San Jacinto, are around the valley, making perfect frame for its fair beauty. Under the winter rains the fields became green for a little, but when the cloudless days came on, speedily the great brown mantle of desert waste spread over the entire scene. Brave men — a leader among whom was Judge North — came and saw how finely these great plains were sheltered by the mountain walls, and fancied, if they could but bring the water from the hills, they could change this desert to a garden. They found the springs of the rivers in the hills, and bravely made their ditches; carried on sprawling legs of timber their flumes across the valleys, and poured the might of water into the desert's lap. The soil laughed with flowers, the vine flourished, the almond-tree whitened in the sun; and from old New England, and the later New England in the fair northwest, came colonists, not poor in purse or brain, but strong-handed, brave-hearted, large-brained men. They reared their little cottages, planted their vineyards, put in their seedlings, and, digging their ditches, sat down to watch the miracle of the water coaxing from the soil the wonders of its latent life. The valley between the mountains smiled with beauty, and began to wave its orange plumes to the hills from whence came its strength; the ditches were extended yet beyond; others heard of the marvel here; farther towards the mountains vineyard and orchard ran; flowers were sown, trees along the way were planted, not for fruitage, but for beauty's sake; and wherever the magic water could be made to flow, there the miracle of growth was acted, until, after years so few that they are spanned by the memory of those who are but children yet, the place which was the valueless ranch of the herder has become

> "The land where the lemon-trees bloom,
> Where the gold orange grows in the deep thicket's gloom,
> Where a wind ever soft from the blue heavens blows,
> And the groves are of laurel and myrtle and rose."

Never did tourists journey with wider-opened eyes or with larger haste. How gladly would we loiter here and there, dreaming in quiet villages, musing beside the sea, waiting listlessly and aimlessly while Nature transfers to the canvas of our minds her masterpieces! Of all the days spent in the Old World, none linger so pleasantly with us as those quiet ones, when for hours we sat and dreamed beside fair lakes and in the midst of old historic scenes; and it is our grievous misfortune now that for days and weeks together we cannot loiter, dream, and linger, until the very life and atmosphere of the scenes we see shall become part of our very souls. And yet we are loitering here. We came for the interval of the trains; we have passed the day, we are on the second day; and so are the enchantments of Riverside affecting us, that when we rose this morning, remembering the rare evening we had passed, sitting amid the roses in the dewless night, with the moon's

"Level rays like golden bars,"

and looked out on a day so fair, seeing the world

"Smiling as if the earth contained no tomb,"

we were not surprised to find that the spur of our resolution had lost its power, that we no longer were solicitous for moving on, and without a word of protest, said, "Yes, we will stay another day," though we know that we must purchase staying by sacrifice of some wonder, for seeing which we have the ticket in our pocket.

We can feel now, as we never felt before, the story of the "Lotus Eaters," who, under the spell of the delightful scenes through which they journeyed, forgot home and country, and were content to loiter ever in the lotus land. We have actually taken the pictures of our little family and placed them close beside us, to use them as a charm to break the spell, not only of this fair region, but of the fast-increasing friends who are weaving swiftly the enchantments of their hospitality over our poor yielding and delighted soul. Already fruit from orchard and field has been brought to us; busy men have changed their plans of labor that they might wait upon us; and not one, but many, have brought wives and children to sit with us in the moonlight of these perfect nights amid the roses of the doll-house, which is our friend's home.

We cannot understand how these fair scenes have come. Surely there has been some sorcery that has evolved these wonders,— trees of lordly girt, lawns green with a turf knit seemingly by years of growth, changing the plain into a vast park of many miles in area. The village is small: a few stores, churches, a public hall, a newspaper, of course, the matchless "Glenwood," a hotel superbly kept, a few homes set around with trees,— this is the village, though it should be said that there is within it cleanliness, order, and large sobriety. From the village outward are cypress hedges close beside the zanjas, with cactus plants and blooming flowers all along beside the road, and far extending backward row on row of orange-trees,— oh, so green and beautiful!— hundreds, thousands; with lemon, walnut, peach, nectarine, apricot, and pomegranate; with great flaming plants and delicate roses round the houses, and such roads and walks and long vistas among the trees as make one feel that these things are not for the occupation, but only for the amusement, of their owners. We have scant taste for details of figures: we only know that grapes are gathered by the ton, and oranges sent to market by the thousand; that we have seen presses for the raisin, and have eaten muscats and muscatels, fig and peach and pear, until we shudder for the fermentation that will ensue when we strike the heat of the southern desert to-morrow on our journey.

The land sold here only a few years ago for thirty-five, is now valued at a thousand, dollars; and probably in all the country there is nowhere so fair a colony as this, wrought out of the desert by the brawn of labor and the brain of intelligence. We have been charmed with the people we have met. Seldom have we seen keener men, full of public spirit, believers in the future of Riverside, — men who have achieved something, and regard no obstacle as insuperable. Eastern capital abounds, and seldom has it happened when wealthy people have stayed for a time that they have not made their home here among the orange groves.

We have written by our chamber window far into the night, and to-morrow at an early hour a new-made friend comes to carry us out, before the going of the stage, to pluck orange blossoms from the tree. Then onward to the desert, of which men have spoken with such words of pity. To-morrow night we shall be at Yuma, to which place, it is said, the dead natives come back from Hades when they are frozen out. Then on to Mexico for a little, thence to Colorado, and to the summit of Pike's Peak on a donkey's back, thence homeward once again.

We draw the curtain ere we drop our pencil for one last look upon the beauty of this perfect night; even the voices of the night are hushed, and the orange-trees sleep in the light without the rustle of a leaf. We wonderingly ask ourselves, Why is it that these days and nights have brought such beauty to us? Is it because really the flowers are of deeper hue, the trees of fairer foliage, than elsewhere in our journeys? Or is it because the hunger of the heart for human friendliness has, after all these days of wandering, found here at last a place where friendship could speak its kindly word, and loving sympathy extend its tender offices? After all, Nature in all her varied moods touches only the surface of our life. We wonder and we worship in her temples; but there is no touch of sympathy in rock or wood, and we starve even in Nature's wonder-places for the humanity that belongs to life and love.

There is somewhere a legend of Ceylon that he who has once set foot upon its soil and leaves it, wanders through the world with a vague and melancholy discontent which cannot be appeased until he has returned. We have no doubt that, until we reach kind friends again, we shall long with unutterable yearning for this cosey cottage-room in the moonlight here beneath the vines, and have fair visions of the orange groves and cypress-shaded avenues of this fair colony. And in the coming days, when in the old home we have around us the old friends and the old loves, we are certain that we shall even then remember this oasis here on the desert's edge, and the new friendships formed beneath the orange leaves.

# ACROSS THE DESERT.

*What thy soul holds dear, imagine it
To lie that way thou go'st.*
                              SHAKSPEARE.

# CHAPTER XI.

### ACROSS THE DESERT.

IT is three days' journey across the great southern Territories to Colorado. Friends at home pitied us when we told them of our route of travel, and wondered why we did not choose the central way instead of this path across the desert. But everybody went the middle way. We had heard of it and read of it, until we knew it all by heart, and we had desire to see the strange life of a less hackneyed region. We confess, too, that there was a fascination in the thought of going out by the northern pines, and returning by the way of the sunny South, with its orange groves and cactus flowers.

The transition from Southern California to the desert is rapid. Under the San Bernardino range the orange-trees thrive, and there is the rich luxuriance which comes where the water flows. But when the zanjas stop, then begins the desert.

Hardly is the old mission town of Bernardino out of sight before we pass into the great basin where, beyond tradition's memory, there was a vast lake. It is two hundred and fifty feet below the level of the sea, and the very hottest place upon the continent. It is a cold day when we pass through, the mercury having dropped from the boiling-point to the mildly tepid stage of one hundred and two degrees. Even this is reasonably sultry, although the brakemen tell us that on an average day they are obliged to wear gloves when they touch the brakes. We notice, however, that the natives here have the luxuriant imagination peculiar to the tropics; and we do not literally accept all their alleged facts, although we do not deny their statement, that to this place their dead friends come back from Hades when they are frozen out.

Passing through this tropic belt the way has many attractions. All the way across there are mountain ranges of rare beauty of outline, finely cut, with such sharp lines as we have never seen. They have no sign of vegetation, but look as if the great lava sea had stiffened into rock. So deeply are they indented, that they appear to be filled with caverns, and, with the long plains before and the cloudless sky above, they are such things as we imagine the mountains of Moab must be.

Towards the east the mountains soften into soil, with great sloping sides and little uplands lying pleasantly upon them.

Crossing the Colorado River we are in Arizona, "the treasure-chest" of the continent. The waters of the river are muddy, and there is faint trace here at Yuma of the wonders of scenery that lie along the course of its upper waters. The town is rude, made of adobe; every nationality is represented at the train, Mexican herders from the ranches, miners, prospectors, tourists. A band of vagrant Yuma Indians are here, with splendid hair, but, oh! with so little clothing on.

The day is perfect as we speed across the Territory. The scenery is monotonous, of course, but having many attractions for one who has eyes to see. The cactus is everywhere, growing in broad-leaved branches or in great masses of spiky vegetation. The land towards the eastern border is richer, softer, greener. In the Gila valley it is even beautiful, for recent rains have brought the water for miles beside the track, brown and rich in color. So softly does the light rest on this, that the little wire upon the poles is reflected in it.

Cattle are feeding now upon the plains, and between our windows and the distant hills we see, from time to time, great wagon-trains moving with slow-paced oxen always toward the west. A rare mirage delights us. A lake, placid as the Revelator's sea of glass, seems to lie there in the west; and in the lake are islands, great, dome-like mounds, little sylvan spots floating on the waters, and larger masses, green with sloping fields, —

> "Sister isles, that seem to smile
> Together, like a happy family,
> Of beauty and of love."

So real is it, that we cannot persuade ourselves that it is only a mirage, until after the vision passes.

New Mexico has larger fertility than Arizona. Civilization has not yet reached its limit here. Sheriff Tucker, we learn, has killed eight men thus far in the season since the first of May, and seventeen murders have taken place in Deming since that time.

At one of the stations two prospectors take the cars. They have been out for months, riding in the saddle by day, sleeping under the stars by night, on the open plains; and they tell us of old Toltec cities toward the south, where, centuries ago, strange houses were built by a race now vanished, of great mounds filled with rude weapons and pottery of finer art than any living tribe has fashioned. There are few towns along the way; but while the plains are desert-like with their neutral tints, beyond them are the great ranges, soft with hues of purple and golden mist.

As we come north the towns begin to multiply, set in the midst of cotton-woods, green with the irrigating waters from the hills; and now the natives point out the sites of old mines from which in other days large treasure was obtained. For centuries, after the rude fashion of those days, these mines were worked, then abandoned, until recent enterprise has opened them again, and, with larger capital, is bringing out abundant wealth. Here at San Marcial the battle of Valvercle was fought in 1862; at Socorro are the famous Torrence and Merritt mines; and all the mountains here are showing richest prospects. Set here in the plains is the city of Albuquerque. It is only three years old, but it has ten thousand people, and boasts its electric lights and telephones.

At Wallace we are on historic ground, for here in 1693 Gen. Diego de Vargas made encampment with his army, and here the revolution against the crown ended, the rebellious Indians making submission to the king, having received the promise that they should no longer work within the mines, and that the covered shafts should not again be opened.

At Los Cerrillos is the old Spanish Mina del Tierra, noted two hundred years ago as the richest mine upon the globe. It was worked by Indians, who climbed on a rude terrace-like causeway of notched poles, to the surface, bearing the ore in bags made of skins. Near this mine is one of the old chalchinti, or turquoise mines, from which part of the jewels of the Spanish crown were taken. The refusal of the Indians to work in this mine led to a general revolution, in which the Spaniards were defeated and driven from the country.

At some of the stations we met the Pueblo Indians; they are a stupid set, not over-clean, ignorant of English, not over-modest in their dress.

We visit Santa Fé, because everybody goes to this city. It is said to be rich; if so, it is exceedingly modest in its display. It is old, if that is an advantage. It has public buildings, but they are insignificant; some old churches, made of mud; a few picturesque streets. But the adobe houses are at best poor things; they do not satisfy the artistic sense, though they are regarded as a good card in this city, which makes merchandise of its antiquity. We could not keep from our mind the unclassical words of Finnegan's song, —

> "Our fathers had castles of mud,
> Of which they were fond of admiring;
> They were built in the time of the flood,
> For to keep all our ancestors dry in."

We are to leave the cars at an early hour in the morning, and are therefore in the common car. We are but few in number, and have made good arrangements for the night. But at Trinidad a change comes over the spirit of our dreams, for the fire company of Pueblo enters, returning from a tournament in which it has been victorious. Each man bears a broom, and we are overwhelmed, as though an army of locusts had come. The average member of an ordinary hand-engine is not docility personified: a member of a Western company takes on new graces; a Western company returning at midnight from a tournament bearing the champion's belt is some degrees more demoralizing than a Minnesota blizzard. Life becomes a burden; it soon becomes an apprehension, for a reckless passenger in the forward car drawing his revolver calls down upon himself the wrath of the Pueblo heroes returning with victorious spoils. The man of arms is not a hero, and, retreating before the wrath he has inflamed, he comes to the car we occupy, to bear there from time to time, with great abjectness, the revilings of the bullies he has roused but dares not silence.

So escorted, we cross the boundaries of the Centennial State, and are soon domiciled in the pleasant villages beneath the snow-clad peaks of Colorado.

# A MEXICAN DÉTOUR.

*Shall we go see the relics of this town?*
                                        SHAKSPEARE.

## CHAPTER XII.

#### A MEXICAN DÉTOUR.

CROSSING the Rio Grande, we feel at once the atmosphere of another and older empire. The Texan city of El Paso, on the northern side, is alive with the stir of enterprise; but El Paso del Norte slumbers yet, feeling only slightly the coming in of the new life of commerce which is so soon to change the old kingdom of Montezuma substantially into another American State. The horse-cars between the two cities bring us between narrow garden-walls covered with thick traceries of vine to the depot of the Ferrocarril Central Mexicano. Dark-eyed boys stand idly here and brown-faced natives, while at the windows of the cars are not over-comely faces peering at each new arrival with that curiosity which belongs to the gentler sex.

The day of revolutions is over, in Northern Mexico at least. The wild Apache's reign has passed, and nowhere is life more secure than along the road southward to the city of Chihuahua. Nevertheless, the government compels the carrying of a guard of twenty native soldiers; and here they come, — swarthy, shambling, unsocial fellows, clad in loose summer clothes, not over-jaunty in their style, and officered by a young lieutenant, ungracious and unkempt, not out exactly at the elbows, but at other parts not less conspicuous. The road has been built by New England enterprise, a most generous subsidy being granted by the government. Massachusetts officers are in charge; the pay-roll bears for the most part good old names familiar in the New England towns; and if beyond the needs of the high officials there is a remnant left for the common holders of the stock, without a doubt they must carry their coupons to State Street to get their cash.

Due south, two hundred and twenty-five miles, Chihuahua lies. For fifty miles the road passes over a vast sandy plain, unrelieved, save in the northern portion, where in the distance the Rio Grande is seen winding in the east amid the verdure created by its waters. The soil is dry, covered with a scanty growth of mesquite and cactus, and the cattle feeding here are of the wild and wiry kind. The Mexican steer has a not over-enviable reputation in our city streets, because of a somewhat excessive agility; but in his native fields here along the track, he must be indeed an agile creature if he would find sufficient forage to keep him in condition.

Soon the Candelarian Range looms up, great peaks

of every curious form, softened by the pleasant haze of this delicious air, changing southward into round *buttes* and peaks, rising from the plains as fair as old Ascutney from its New England meadows; and between the hills are pleasant valleys, bringing down their soft verdure even to the desert's edge; while over all the scene great cloud-masses begin to form and move, tinged at the closing of the day with rarest colorings. The cattle now multiply, for we are crossing the vast ranches of the cattle kings, and from these distant hills come down the streams that fertilize the plains; no village is along the way, and slight sign of habitation, save the cottages of the ranchmen, with cattle corral set round with cotton-woods. Once we pass a little group of travelling natives taking their siesta in the shade of the station water-tank, the little burros feeding near, and such rare groupings of children and draperies of dress and coverings as an artist would have envied.

Central Mexico, in its entire length, is a desert, save where irrigation has brought fertility. Along the coast, where there is the moisture of the sea, there is tropical luxuriance of growth; but here it is treeless, almost verdureless, and were it not for the royal hills and the majestic clouds, our journey southward would be exceedingly monotonous.

We have been journeying now over the great ranch of Governor Terrazas. At the little stations skilful horsemen have given surprising exhibitions of their skill; family groups have joined us, going to the city for the Sabbath fête; and the resplendent cowboy, armed like an arsenal, and covered with the costly sombrero, which, beyond wife or horse or even arms, is cherished as the one immediate jewel of the cowboy's soul. The Mexican is not loquacious. Silent even with each other, we wonder if behind these dark eyes there is not just a hint of enmity at these palefaced strangers who have come to change the empire of his fathers? The mountains round the city are tinged with sunset colors as we reach our journey's end, the white walls are softened, and the great twin-towered temple, which is the glory of Chihuahua, stands in the midst, as though the city purposely had been built beneath its cathedral walls.

Around the station the scene is marvellous in its details of life. Mexican carriages mingle with the latest-fashioned vehicles, men and women upon horseback, children upon burros, the modern omnibus with its gaudy colors, Indians, natives, foreigners of every dialect, — all are here; and every costume, from the half-clad Indian and Mexican with fringe and spur and sash, to the latest fashion from the States, — all mingling here; while on the hills the setting sun is kindling its evening fires, and beyond in the soft light sits between the mountains the white city, like some old Moorish town. The old and new civilizations meet here, — the adobe walls of the city and the iron railway of the North, the Indian, Spaniard, and the Anglo-Saxon; just there beyond, the new car is being put upon the tramway, while, moving onward to the city, march off with shambling gait the silent guard that has journeyed with us from the North.

Upon the highest perch of the loftiest coach we ride into the city. How strange it is! Women washing at the little stream beside the road; curious streets, bounded with houses which seem to be but walls, and long lanes running hitherward, thitherward, with barracks for the soldiers, and little stores, some absolutely windowless; quaint signs in Spanish above the doors; dark eyes looking at us from latticed windows; and in the streets women walking under the shadow of the walls, with Spanish lace deftly thrown above their shapely heads with that rare coquetry which has belonged to woman since Adam was born with eyes to see.

We are at the Plaza now, and at the one American hotel the city has we find our quarters. Toward the street it is, like all these houses, most unpretentious. You enter through an archway an open court flagged with stone, and by a winding way come to a corridor running round this court. Here is the room that we shall have; windowless, save as the lattice of the door is window, with floor of stone, iron bedsteads, and just that tinge of color set off with blue that one sees in Northern Italy, among the lakes, in little hostelries and villa houses. We have no sort of spite against the easy-going landlord who carries on the house by proxy through his colored porter. We hope our duster fitted the husband of the chambermaid who kleptomanied it; and when the rainy season comes, we trust the waiters' aprons will be put out to catch the drippings of the showers. We have an appetite not readily adjustable, we fear, to the Mexican style of living. The dishes are not always dried, and a kind of soap-sud flavor is carried over by them to the gravies of the succeeding meal, and there is slight over-use of garlic, and withal such a general over-doing of the meats and an under-doing of the fish, that we feel that somehow David Garrick must have been dining here when he said that "Heaven sends meat, but the devil sends cooks."

The city of Chihuahua contains, perhaps, twenty thousand souls. It has an honorable history, for here Hidalgo was confined and executed, and the cathedral tower bears marks yet of the invasion of Maximilian. The streets are of generous width, swept clean in the early morning of every day with brooms of green willow boughs. The houses are of adobe, though some of the public buildings are of stone. The roofs are flat, and toward the street there is great monotony in these endless walls of garish stone; and as one walks the streets in the early morning, before the life of the city stirs, he feels that he would die were he compelled to look for a single month on these long walls. There is one great street called the Alameda, running backward to the hills. Trees flourish, and seats of stone are beneath their branches. It is wide beyond all others. Here, on Sabbath days, the military band plays before the evening concert in the Plaza, and on great fête days the people gather to see the Virgin's image pass, borne on by priests. Market, City Hall, cathedral, gather around the Plaza, which is the heart of Chihuahua. To-morrow is the Sabbath, and there is a larger stir than usual in the market square. The market building is pierced by archways on every side, and entering in we see a strange scene. The Placita, or inner court, is open to the sky, and the full moon is struggling behind great clouds, throwing into ominous shadow these strange faces crouching above their little stores. Black eyes flash beneath broad sombrero brims; on frail stands and barrels these tradesmen have their goods, and on the pavement, beside heaps of fruit, women sit, their faces strangely colored in these cross lights; on the laps of weary mothers children sleep, while, unsolicited, lest the sleepers wake, the buyers pass up and down.

In and out among them, threading our way over the withered fruits of these belated sellers, we gaze and wonder at the weirdness of the scene, — these strange faces, draped in these Rembrandt shadows, the utter weariness which had come from many hours of watching, the flickering lights in rude lanterns, the strange fruits, the stranger language of passing buyers. The stock in trade is pitifully meagre, and those who buy take with them tiniest purchases; for these people here have learned to make their necessities miserably few, and the city has no middle class, but only the rich and poor.

The very weirdness of the place attracts us, and when, late at night, wearied with long journeyings in the streets, we come back to hear the music of the fountain's play within the Plaza, we are drawn again to the market-place close by. The group of sellers has thinned a little, for it is nearly midnight, and only now and then does some tardy housewife come for the morrow's store; but still patiently sit these humble toilers. The shadows deepen in the paler light, while on the mother's lap sleep on the little ones, as happy as if the world would bring no care.

The streets contain the people now, for it is a summer's night. Around the drinking-places are little groups of men, and at the archways house-wives are stopping for the gossip of the day; through the barred windows we see fair rooms hung round with pictures, and in not a few some signs of luxury; through the archways are visible the quiet

Placitas set round with flowers, while in the dewless air fathers play with children or friends gather for social joys. Hearing the sound of music, we listen beneath the windows, and shabby though it is, so curious are we, we climb a little so that we can overlook the shutters and see within. A group of boys are gathered round a teacher, who, with much vociferation and some angry words, if we can judge aright, is making rehearsal for the cathedral service of the morrow; and very sweet, too, sound these youthful voices chanting the service of the Holy Church in the pleasant measures of the Spanish speech.

As the evening changes into night, mothers are making beds before their doors for their little ones; and so thick, as the night wears on, become these sleepers in the street, that we almost fear to walk among them, so angrily have the black eyes of those who guard them flashed at us.

There is no more unfailing source of pleasure than to see a great city wake to life. But Chihuahua wakes not as other cities, with gradually increasing noise and stir. The cathedral bells call to early Mass, and we can hear the footsteps of the worshippers without. From the corridor of the Placita the servant calls with drawling tones to the morning meal; and while the fountain plays within the Plaza, and around it women are filling their water-jars there is no other token that another day has come.

We go up and down the streets, sit beneath the branches of the Alameda, see the little burros coming in, bearing in panniers milk and comforts for the day, — not seldom bearing, too, great stalwart men urging on their beasts with peculiar never-ceasing shaking of the knees, as though the palsy were the epidemic of the nation. Great lines of burros bring wood upon their backs and sides; most curious wood it is, — branches curled and twisted, gnarled into such knotty curvatures as if in the night some one had stripped the trees that Doré used to be so fond of picturing in his forests.

We hope it is because of no morbid passion for sight of wretchedness, nor yet because of any anticipating of our fate, that we have interest in the prison of the city; but here we are at the iron gate, and on the wrong side of it are twenty fellows who would exchange places with us and make short dicker with the trade. The city is phenomenal in its order; while the police are such strange fellows, — so armed and girded with weapons of every kind, so clumsy by reason of accoutrement, that a rogue of facetious temperament would surely die with laughter at his captor; yet the city is in perfect order, and has bad eminence with the unruly classes. We find some Americans waiting here who tell sad tales of hardships. They are in prison through the failure of the authorities to rightly interpret some unfortunate circumstances in which they were unhappily engaged; they speak disparagingly of the Mexican character, and are not hearty in praise of the institutions of the Republic. Notwithstanding their apparent flesh, they are wasted, they assert, with insomnia because of the tarantulas which infest the cells; and if we will get them out, and in the mean time give them some tobacco, we shall be doing a favor to fellow-countrymen who are temporarily in trouble.

The Church of St. Francisco is the oldest church within the city. It is rude in architecture, and has no grace that it should be desired. The interior decorations are poor and tawdry; the altar-rail painted green, the gates a little saggy at the hinges; the arch behind is veneered with carved wood placed in sections; here are poorly painted panel pictures, all awry, an altar decorated like the playhouse of a child, tinsel flowers in china vases, and looking-glasses, with fire-screens behind tallow dips, and such utter childishness of ornament that one is saddened at the spectacle. There are most grotesque and hideous figures of the Saviour, with blood-stained, agonizing face, with all the repulsiveness of suffering, and none of the grandeur which some of the old masters used to show.

The confessional is ruder than in any of the churches we have seen; and here beside the altar in the Virgin's chapel is the repulsive bier, waiting for the burial of the dead. A mother and daughter are crooning here their prayers, keeping tally with their beads. From altar to altar they pass, kissing altar cloths and rails, and even the pavement of the floor, — the mother brusque and business-like, but the daughter inclined to linger, much freer with her glances at the strangers than seems consistent with the spirit of devotion.

The Cathedral crowns the city. Go where you will, its towers always are in sight. Built nearly two hundred years ago by taxation of the Santa Eulalia Silver Mine, it is associated with the tenderest experiences of the people's life. It is of Moorish architecture; built of adobe, with towers faced with stone not unlike in color the Parisian buildings. The front is of most elaborate workmanship, with fluted pillars rising one above the other, with figures of the saints set in niches everywhere, the whole covered with delicate arabesques, like the fine chasings on a jewel; and flanking this façade are massive towers, severely plain in their lower parts, that nothing may detract from the rich entrance-way which they enclose, but blossoming out above the gable of the façade into tapering spires set round with fluted pillars rising in marvellous symmetry to the shining crosses set against the sky.

The walls are but poorly fashioned, having only such poor grace as art can fashion of adobe with slight mixture of rubble-stone, with bungling attempt at beauty in flying buttresses upon the roof, and a heavy dome surmounted by an iron cross most sadly out of plumb. The eastern portal, however, is of surpassing beauty, — so rich in gentle traceries that one might fancy that a section of the old Alhambra had been transported here, with fair Corinthian pillars and imaged saints set round with beauty. The interior disappoints. The wooden timbers of the roof are sadly out of place, and there is lacking here the massiveness, the tender grace of the cathedrals of the older world; while the windows are set high, with no symmetry of form or richness of color. There is great poverty of decoration; the altar is a faded thing, and even the vestments of the priests are common; while the music, which is the soul of the service of the Church, is thin and strident, stirring no emotion. The High Mass of the Sabbath is in progress, and the vast edifice is filled with kneeling forms.

The type of face is purely native; here and there the clean-cut features of the Spaniard can be seen, and the darker shade of the native Indian; but the Mexican face prevails, telling in the rugged lines that life here has been not wholly a thing of idle dreams. Miner, merchant, ranchmen from the hills, all are here, with curious costumes merging slowly into the Anglo-Saxon type that is to be the fashion of the world. There are but few fair faces in the multitude of women, although most cleverly have these cunning hands set them round with frame of gentle folds of shawl and scarf. One face within the kneeling crowd attracts us, not by reason of its loveliness, but because of its fair white color and such rapt ecstasy of worship as the pictures of the saints sometimes wear. The priest most famous in the city preaches, with such surprising eloquence that though we understand no word of Spanish we are greatly moved.

As night comes on, the glory of the Plaza is revealed. The great cathedral towers stand sentinel above it in this rare moonlight, and from all the city streets the throngs are coming to keep the Sabbath fête around the fountain. The little hucksters are setting up their wares and lighting the lanterns of their stalls, and parents leading children come, and fair señoritas go round and round the Plaza's circle, while in the centre the military band plays with vigor if not with skill. It is said that in one of the Colorado churches there is posted this notice: "Please don't shoot the organist; he is doing the best he can." We hardly think that this entreaty would save these fellows if these throngs had large sense of music; but the air is balmy, and in quiet converse, and such gentle fellowships as men and women make, the evening wears on till eleven o'clock, when the music stops, and no sign of life remains save the fountain playing in the light and the watchman making his weary rounds.

We seek in the earlier evening the one Protestant service of the city. It is not an easy thing to find a place in these streets which are so alike. The people backward from the larger stores are not versed in English speech, and so we try as best we can to tell our errand in such Spanish as we had learned in the visit of the day. We do not half succeed, we fear, for, following the direction which our question brings, we find ourselves at a hotel, which is not a church at all. We find the place at last, a preacher's home, but miss the hour of service. We are met in the Placita by a fair New Jersey girl, who loves to talk of this strange city and of the old home by the far Atlantic. In the midst of our pleasant converse a child's voice cries out, "Auntie, I want my pills!" and we can but say, "We never saw before a boy that cried for pills!"

We have a long audience with the mayor, a gentleman of most engaging speech and kindly ways. He tells us of the city, of the patriot Hidalgo, of the reign of law that had been brought into the city, of the grander life that is coming to the old nation with the progress of the railway and the coming in of new ideas. He has kindliest wishes for the Northern strangers who are changing the old into the new, but grieves that capital should so be squandered by reckless men. "We have," he says, "worked our mines for ages. In rude fashion, if you please, but always to advantage. Your people come; our ways are wrong to them; costly machinery is bought; the old overseers are unheeded, and men ignorant of our customs and our people, ignorant of mining even, are put in charge, wealth is squandered, and no profit comes." The government of the city is carefully administered; the people are content; the coming in of American capital has improved the condition of the laboring classes, and despite the excessive tariff the stores are filled with the products of American shops and looms. The men are reasonably well educated, while the condition of woman is degraded, in that she is regarded as the toy and drudge of man, rather than his companion. We see but little of the gallantry we supposed belonged to this people, and the sad faces which peer at us from beneath the soft folds of the little shawls which cover the heads with such consummate grace still haunt us. The death of children under ten is esteemed not grievous, and for the dead of every age there is not that tenderness of memory, nor care to make beautiful the place of burial, which belongs to some other nations. The city still retains in the architecture of its streets, its pleasant language, its laws and customs, the peculiar flavor of the past. Not in a day does a new civilization impose itself upon a people. But the strong, at last, make the laws and life of the weak; and commerce is to do for Mexico what the conquest of arms could not do, — change the language and the very spirit of the people.

As we turn our face northward, we rejoice that before the transition comes which shall merge this people into the great Northern life, we have seen the city and felt the movement of the old life of ages. And so we leave behind the music of the Plaza's fountain, and the fair temple which holds aloft its splendid towers, like the brooding of an angel's wings, over the fair city of Chihuahua.

*But on and up, where Nature's heart
Beats strong amid the hills.*
MILNES.

## CHAPTER XIII.

### COLORADO DAYS.

THE gateway of Colorado is the city of Pueblo. Here the roads diverge, going northward to Denver, westward to the Gunnison Country and Salt Lake, with a line between extending to Leadville.

We will first go Denverward forty-five miles, stopping at Colorado Springs. The intervening space is unattractive; the land is bare, with few signs of either vegetable or human life. As we draw near our destination in the West, a great line of mountains stands against the sky, culminating in the towering summit of Pike's Peak. It is hard to conceive of any mountains such as these being without beauty, but this great wall of stone is seamed and scarred with such grand lines, there is such massiveness of outline, rock and forest so cleverly intermingle, that even the first view fascinates and enchants. What Interlaken is to the Jung Frau, such is Colorado Springs to Pike's Peak. Seated upon the plateau on which the town rests, we are at just the proper focal distance, — a little near, perhaps, but not too far to catch the grace of the intervening meadow and the beauty of the little valleys that run among the hills. This Colorado sky is something wonderful, — deep, rich, magnificent. The colors of field and mountain are strangely brilliant; and nowhere on the continent have we found a place where, with larger content, we could sit all through the summer days and watch the sun and clouds paint their pictures on the everlasting hills.

Shrewd enterprise laid the foundation of Colorado Springs. The town is a model of thrift and beauty; streets of metropolitan dimensions, public buildings of taste, private homes placed in the midst of gardens, while the purest water carries health through all the town.

To the world Colorado Springs contains the attractions of this region, and there is no great attempt on the part of the natives of the place to undeceive. But beyond the view, and the beauty of a thrifty village, there is nothing here. Even the springs, from which the town is named, are five miles away, at Manitou. From this smaller place the trail leads to the summit of Pike's Peak, while around the quiet village nestle such beauties as decorate few places in any land. But alas for Manitou! the steam-presses of the newspapers are at the pretentious town yonder across the valley, and the strangers disembark at the latter place and stay, until, visiting the lovely village five miles away, they give their hearts to Manitou. And it is incomparable in beauty. A quiet little spot dropped among the hills, with pleasant roads, and winding lovers' paths beside the singing stream, with cottages vine-embowered, pleasant hillside homes, and such romantic roads leading to wonder-places, that one could spend a summer here and not exhaust the charm of this fair Manitou.

Even now it seems to us as a pleasant summer's dream, for heaven and earth seem to kiss each other here. And how shall we describe a dream? Or where shall we begin to tell of the beauties of a perfect picture, or put in words the rhythm of a matchless poem? and Manitou is dream, picture, poem, all in one, the loveliest spot that nestles anywhere among the fairest valleys of the continent.

The town is a tiny thing. A few hotels, the village houses not obtrusive, summer cottages nestling beside the river and on the hills, little colonies of tents where the campers are, the Casino, with its pleasant architecture, the winding road beside the river, and over all the majestic mountains,— this is Manitou; and yet this is not all, for there is a nameless witchery that eludes description, an atmosphere which words cannot picture, a subtle grace that baffles speech. Was there ever such royal afternoon as this on which we start to make exploration of the beauties that are here?

The stables of the village shelter no finer, fleeter horse than this we ride, for, with the utmost courtesy that we can use, we search and find the softest spot in the owner's heart; and does he not know by the look within our eyes that we have loyal love for a noble horse? And so we shall have this royal fellow to bear us on our way.

To the Garden of the Gods first.

The stableman tells, with minute directions, just where the wonders are. This stone from such a point is Mrs. Grundy; that, a monk; the other, some peculiar wonder, we know not what.

There is but little doubt that the fantastic stones do assume the shapes described, and that, by a happy exercise of faith and vision, one can see strange forms in this museum of nature. There is little doubt, too, that the average tourist is so intent on finding these monstrosities, that he misses the grandeur and glory of the place. We have seen so much seeking of the infinitely little in the midst of the infinitely great, that we are in chronic revolt against the simply curious; we have come to abominate freaks of nature, and so we will not even look for a single resemblance in rock or cliff.

We do not wonder that writers visiting this place, beguiled by the emphasis placed upon its fantastic freaks, should have missed somewhat the larger beauty of the Garden of the Gods. It is a wonder-place, not in freaks and fantastic carvings, but in the great red peaks that guard its entrance; in its superb coloring of rock and cliff; the pleasant vales of verdure; the gigantic sculpturings; and over all the majestic glory of Pike's Peak, throned like a monarch above the hill and plain.

In the upper part of this strange valley, through a rustic gateway, we enter fair Glen Eérie. The hills bound it in on either side; and, following up a little stream broken into bits of beauty by a thousand tiny falls, we come into the very heart of the hills. How beautiful and majestic, too, are these rounded summits, these beetling crags, these fair slopes garnitured with flowers and foliage! It is the very holy of holies of the hills; and surely Nature has lavished here the utmost riches of her skill!

But along the way there is beauty, too; for the road winds like a serpent's trail, the branches are interbraided in leafy canopies above our heads, and rare traceries of vines, crimsoned with such glory as the autumn brings, garland the forest trees; by the brookside and in little bits of meadow brilliant flowers grow, tinted with the barbaric color that wildness loves, while in the tiny places where the winding of the brook has made a tongue of land, kindly art has planted flowers fenced round with curious stones like grotto walls. So through such leafy arch as we have never seen, with flowers broidering the way, we wind in and out among the beauties of fair Glen Eérie, wondering how in this far-off region, which only a little time ago was an undiscovered land, nature and art have so wondrously wrought to make among the hills one of the earth's loveliest places. While the lights and shadows weave royal tapestries upon our path, canopied with foliage, we commune in delightful silence with the spirit of Glen Eérie, with nothing to break the spell of its enchantment save the tread of our horses' feet, and the low, sweet music of the running stream. Backward to the town, through it and beyond, we ride on and up into the rugged wildness of the old Ute Pass. Had we the finer vision, we might, dismounting, find perhaps the old tracks of the Ute warriors who used to pass this way. We should surely find traces of the pioneers who, in the delirious days of gold, came here to find fortune in the gulches of the hills, and from our saddle we can now see the ruts worn by the supply trains of the great camps beyond among the mountains, — for this is the Leadville trail; and, while our panting steed stands here above the gorge, we hear the tinkling bell of the long wagon-trains climbing by this rugged way to their destination among the summits. It is a wild, desolate path, — hewn out of the mountain's side, with black overhanging crags, and torrent foaming far below; with graceful falls, and long, sloping, foamy rapids; with curious windings where the hills have indentations; with little caverns into which we can drive our horses and let them drink out of the mountain's heart. There are also great steep pitches of rugged hill running out in little plateaus, as though the road desired resting place, that it might breathe before entering upon another climb.

We must come down the valley to the village, cross the little stream before we enter upon the deep defile of William's Cañon. It is very narrow, hardly more than a trail, though carriages come here by keeping cleverly within the ruts. The cliffs are magnificent; five hundred feet upward they carry their Titanic sculpturings in solitary peaks and pinnacles, superbly colored, moss-stained, weather-marked. Had fair Manitou no other thing than this, it would still have pre-eminence; but this is only one of many wonders, and even here there are stranger things than this defile of rock. There on the face of the cliff, hundreds of feet above the road, is a little opening into the mountain. A narrow path leads to it, and with weariness we will climb to this "Cave of the Winds." Was there ever such wonder as this perched so high towards heaven? One, two, many hundred feet we go into the cliff, to find fantastic halls and banquet chambers, miniature temples with Gothic arches and fair Corinthian pillars, bridal bowers with couches twined with acanthus leaves, grottoes shaped as the hiding-place of nymphs, and such rare fashionings of stalactites as Nature sometimes makes when she has centuries of solitude and darkness in which to toil.

We have come across the continent to climb Pike's Peak, and here the old mountain stands looking in our window at little Manitou all through the night.

We rendezvous in a central place at seven o'clock. A single guide will go with the party, which numbers twelve or more. We have selected the day before the largest horse the stable has; and when we start, in the pleasant gallop to the Iron Spring at which the trail begins, we find that we have made good selection. The inevitable ladies follow on; timid, of course, but full of that high ambition which belongs to those who have never climbed twelve miles toward heaven on a mountain's side. Before the first mile is finished we have left them far behind, thinking perhaps that it will be good manners to go on ahead and see that due arrangements are made for their reception on the summit. The path is a narrow one, but of entrancing beauty. Through groves and fields, on mountain sides, above great precipices, over noisy streams, beside cataract and fall, the path winds on and up. Little glades and glens are passed; rare forest vistas open, long reaches of serpentine paths through tangled grass, fords and meadow roads, rocky trails on lower summits, along the flanks of foothills; for five hours our brave, strong horses bear us to the glory that is on the peak. Meantime the world below seeks to keep us loyal to the beauty that we have left. Whenever we look down and back, new wonders are unfolded. Manitou is lovelier now than ever; the Garden of the Gods, Colorado Springs, the far-extended rolling fields, are at our feet, while all around us are the mountains, — Alps on Alps, — crowned by the fair summit towards which we climb through all the hours.

But our gallant horse has an ambitious rival at his heels, — a large roan beast, who has more than once, we know by his impatience, led the train of horses to the summit. He is bearing a huge, good-natured Irishman, who owns a forge in Cincinnati, — one Patrick Buckley, — a clever-witted fellow, who has rare love of nature, and has travelled much about the earth.

Long ago have we left the slower horses behind, and now the genial Pat and the writer go on together. For two good hours at least we are regaled with such dissertation as Pat can give on "the manly art." Next to love of nature, this fellow has love of fighting. We even think he has had a turn or two within the ring himself; at any rate, he has the record of every pugilist, and talks of Heenan, Sullivan "the Slugger" (whoever he may be), "Tug Wilson," and all the gallant crew of bruisers; giving us such insight into arts of fighting, the rules and regulations of the ring, pools, bets, Marquis of Queensbury rules, and sparring bouts, as we have never had before,— though Pat can hardly understand how one seemingly so intelligent should have lived so long and learned so little.  Meantime we are rising to the summit; among the rocks violets are growing, and such rare golden flowers as we have seldom seen in the valleys that are farther from the sun.  The great billowy mountains of the West are below us now, and the entire State is spread like a map beneath us.  The air is growing thin.  The horses breathe with labor; there are bands like steel tightening around our heads, and the landscape below is strangely changing in our vision.  But we are on the summit now,— a vast field of bowlders, desolate, weird, majestic in its vast altitude above the world.

How far can the vision go? We know not, we care not! What are these peaks eastward, northward? What ranges these, what valleys those? We will not ask, we will not be told. Why should we break this splendid picture into fragments, analyze it into names, dissect glory from glory? The mountains will not lie fairer in the sun because we know the names that belittle them, nor will the ranges add one hue to these golden lines by our knowing what camp or city lies beneath them; the scene shall be unbroken, undesecrated,— an eternal picture hung on memory's walls.

Fifteen thousand feet we are standing now above the level of the sea.  It is not wonderful that we can breathe only with effort; our heads are bursting with severest pains, our lungs heave violently, we stagger as we walk, and only by utmost strain of will can we rouse ourselves to see the glory we have climbed to get.

It is a four hours' journey down to little Manitou from the summit.  But our pugilistic Pat dares us to follow him, if we can.  We will not boast, but we will try.

And so we go down in the wildest race we ever made before.  The charm of mountain travel is in the descent, but it must be a flight rather than a march. The muscles must be relieved from tension, the hands free to catch trees and twigs, and then in great adventurous strides one must go down as the wind goes. Every sense must be alert, eye must not falter, muscles must not fail, the joints must be loyal, and then with a springy, spongy path, with an accomplished tramper to lead or follow, what is there on earth much better than a flight from a mountain's summit to the plains?  But never before have we made such flight on a horse's back!  The road is perilous in places; many times in the ascent did we wonder what would become of us if our horse should make misstep, for half the time we are on narrow trails above precipice and chasm, on frail paths built up of timber, rock, and sand, with narrow causeways and ways so perilous that, on the upward way, climbing with slow, cautious pace, we had need for cool eye and steady hand. This is the path which for twelve miles we are to follow, led by this wild Irish wag. We accept the challenge, and Pat leads on. Shall we ever forget that ride? Down the steeper pitches we can only descend with caution. Miles downward from the summit we must wind among the rocks with slow, painful effort; but when once in the forest, with mad, wild racings, we come down like the wind. Swaying with the quick turnings of the path, half staggering often with suddenly diverging trail, sliding down steep descents of ledge and earth, galloping over level spaces and descending paths alike, so we come down as never men came before that day. Somehow there is intoxication in this mountain air. How otherwise could we come with laughter and mad, swift racings over these dizzy paths, where, hours ago, we walked with trembling; and by what spirit are we possessed that we dare gallop around cliff and bowlder, over narrow bridge, along the mountain's side, where one false step will impale horse and rider on the trees two hundred feet below? But oh, it is a rare, rich ride! Not since the old days has the blood run so swiftly in us, nor since boyhood has there been such exultant life as now, when, with every faculty alive, set firm in stirrup, with every nerve of this stalwart horse quivering responsive to our touch, we come down behind this wild John Gilpin, who would outrun us if he only could.

Men wonder as we pass them in the village, and ask if we have really made the journey to the summit; and even Pat himself, while giving honest praise that he could not defeat us, is surprised to find that in two hours and seventeen minutes we have made the twelve-mile journey, saying nothing of the stop — we will not say how long — outside the town, to let the horses make themselves presentable.

Seventy-five miles northward now to Denver, the marvel city of the West. We cannot believe that only a few years ago it was a desert here, for there are few cities so fair as this. Wise men have laid out this city here: streets of generous width, public buildings of imposing size, private homes of elegance; while from every part of the great place loom up the superb mountain range running one hundred miles or more, with its matchless crest of snow.

We cannot explore all the wonders of this great State, for already the invisible ties that run out from heart to heart begin to draw us back to the old home. We will do the next best thing, and come up here in Jackson's Gallery, and let him show us, in the perfect pictures that this wizard of the camera has made, the glories of the West. So the panorama passes before our vision, — gorges, peaks, mountains, parks, everything that Nature has, every wonder, every glory, from sea to sea, caught on the lenses of this artist's camera, and made by his patient skill into such rare pictures as nowhere in the East have we ever seen.

Going southward now, we will make the journey by night to the Gunnison country, far west, coming back by day and noting the marvels that lie along the way. The city of Gunnison is new, brusque, brisk, large with expectations. Rich mines are in the mountains; and unless the natives lie, — and it is possible they do, — this is to be the richest region in the State.

Leaving the city, coming East, the train bears us straight toward the heart of the hills. The Rocky Mountains are directly in our path, and we are to cross their summit and run with the rivers to the sea. One, two, three engines are put on, — stumpy, determined, unsocial things, with no jewelry of brass or tinsel, but small-wheeled fellows, that will hug the old mountain with tenacious grip, and crawl over it despite its ruggedness. It is a steep task, however, this mountain climb of five thousand feet. When, in twenty years, we shall come this way again with the wings which every traveller will carry then, we shall make this summit in just eight miles; but now we will zigzag up for thirty miles. The road winds not much as yet, but more and more, following the indentations of every valley, skirting precipices, balancing on the side of deep defiles, running around great points of rock, yet clambering in great spirals to the clouds. The tandem-harnessed horses ahead are pulling valiantly, but they do not hurry much. The air is getting thin, perhaps, for they are breathing hard, as we panted when, a month or more ago, we climbed Mount Washburn with our packs. The snow-sheds begin to multiply, great ranges come in view, behind us the road winds like a ribbon below among the trees, and beyond it goes on and on in curious loops and windings, breaking the summit into terraces. Suddenly we stop in the darkness of a vast shed. There is ominous sense of danger. The air is thick with smoke; men go out, loiter upon the steps, go forward but return not, and wonder changes to apprehension. Soon we learn that, with such rude tenderness as men can use, a crushed and mangled workman has been put upon the train, injured in the tunnel just where we stopped in the darkness. He was a laborer upon a construction train moving on the siding. A projecting timber crushed his limbs, and left him maimed and helpless.

But we are on the summit now, and the links are parted. There, a mile below, roll on the little engines, beckoning us to overtake them if we can. We are on the Atlantic Slope, and the afternoon light is making strange shadows in the valleys; and how silently the great peaks lie here midway between the seas below the pomp of moving clouds!

Into the Royal Gorge of the Arkansas we now come. The walls rise three thousand feet, cut into curious forms, fine of line, delicate of color, running up in places with almost invisible traceries, and near by knotted into rough masses as though a molten sea had stiffened into stone. There are openings, too, worn smooth with the melting snows, and here are little tributaries bringing down perpetual streams. Rare surprises of cave and cleft are on these walls, strange channels leading upward to the clouds, old weather scars, and great mosaics of colored rock, with little fringes of fern and grass wherever on shelf of rock there is lodgment for the soil.

Once there flashes at us the verdure of an upward winding valley, soft and green, as sometimes in a nightmare's desolations there will be a glimpse of beauty; and then the crags go on, the shadows deepen, and in great walls, so high that vision almost fails, towers the mass of stone, not beautiful nor wonderful, but simply appalling in majestic awfulness.

So we come back again to Pueblo, and at midnight, fast asleep, we are borne eastward, bearing in our dreams pleasant memories of our Colorado days.

# INCIDENTS OF TRAVEL.

*So comes a reckoning when the banquet's o'er,
The dreadful reckoning ; and men smile no more.*
                                        JOHN GAY.

## CHAPTER XIV.

### INCIDENTS OF TRAVEL.

A ROUND trip across the continent in these prosaic days is not prolific in adventures. The wild Indian, in harmless fashion, eats his rations on the reservation, and Jesse James has gone where the wicked cease from troubling, and even the stage robber is at rest. The only personage who can interject an element of peril into a continental trip is the unromantic cowboy, and there is no absolute certainty that a traveller may be on just the particular train which he "goes through."

We are sorry that we are not able to give to our readers picturesque descriptions of startling perils and heroic instances of personal courage, but in most aggravating security we make our journey, and return home in a state of mortifying safety. But we are not yet home.

Out of the great chasms, leaving behind mountain, gorge, and mine, we come eastward. The fair fields of Kansas and Missouri pass in panorama before us; the Mississippi is crossed, and here we are again at Chicago, safe and sound. Reclining in the easy-chairs with which these enterprising Western roads are furnished, we have time to look around and note the curious life that may be seen even on a railway car. The porter, who responds so readily to the name of John, that we think he must have been christened by it, is in serious trouble all the way. His special function in the world is to keep the way passengers from entering the car. But John's power of resistance is limited, and the amount of personal push and self-assertion developed in these Kansas females is phenomenal. The sable guardian of the through passengers is in a state of chronic altercation, expostulating, remonstrating, threatening, and coaxing, quoting general orders and specific rules, but liable to be overcome by the energetic women, who, though they are riding only between the flag stations, wish to go in as great comfort as the railway company provides for any of its patrons.

A little Massachusetts school-marm, who is going down the road not more than forty miles, comes bouncing in with a perfect avalanche of such bundles as the average woman likes to carry. John advances and guards the passage, but by sheer audacity of speech she overcomes him, and, forcing a passage in, takes a seat behind us, enjoying her journey with the calmest possible serenity. She is utterly oblivious of the fact that she is a voluble little fraud, and that the blushing gentleman on whose chair her not over-dainty feet recline, as well as John, who scowls behind her, know it.

The commercial-traveller genus abounds in these Western States. On the platform of stations where not a house nor store is visible, there is the omnipresent drummer; at lonely water-tanks he screens his head from the noon-day heat beneath the cistern, while he waits for the train; at flag stations he is waving flag or lantern; and go where we may, we hear his hearty laugh and see his good-natured face. We ourselves are even taken for one of the fraternity, and in entering the Colorado City, which bears with us the burden of a not-over comely name, a shabby two-dollar hotel is commended to us, because it has a good sample room and a first-class bar. In several years of travel we have never seen before this day one of these self-reliant fellows seriously annoyed at the ills of life. But now a new experience comes. In the seat just ahead is an ideal specimen of the fraternity. He is arrayed in wonderful expanse of linen, and has that air of proprietorship which belongs to the average over-fed young man. The atmosphere of general omniscience about the fellow awes us; we sit and admire the soft folds of his pulpy neck, really envying his rare capacity for looking wise. The conductor reaches him in the progress of his rounds, and is handed the ticket by the young man with effusive condescension. The official calmly says, "You are on the wrong train."

Language fails to describe the "breaking up" of that drummer; the revelation that he is not omniscient, the utter collapse of dignity, the coming down to the ordinary level of a common, erring, human nature, the descent from the high stilts of his self-conceit of that fat young man, was such a sight as was worth a trip across the continent to see.

We are soon to pass a train returning to Kansas City, and the young man can transfer himself to that and go back his twenty miles. Like the old philosopher, whatever concerns the race is of interest to us, and so we go to the back stairs of the train to see him make the connection. The trains approach, pass, but neither stops. When twenty rods apart they halt, and the fellow launches himself, with his samples. The mercury is warming to its work among the nineties, and it is not easy for a fat man, with half a dozen conscienceless passengers watching, and a box of samples in his hand, to make fast time upon the ties of a railway track. We encourage him with mirthful words, make suggestions as to styles of locomotion; but, despite this help, he fails, for when within arm's length of the train the white rings rise above the engine and the cars move off; and alone upon the track, with samples dropped and pulpy fists shaking east and west at the retreating trains, we leave him with his meditations and his samples.

The traveller across the continent still meets with many curious types of life, although the facilities of travel are fast destroying individual characteristics of costume, speech, and manners. Even in the Territories, frontier life shows the effect of contact with the refinements of the world. There are innumerable comedies, however, on a railway train.

One of our companions finds in the emigrant car a dejected man, who so arouses his sympathy that he makes a canvass of the passengers for help. Every eye is busy with the scenery along the road, and, rather than see his mission absolutely fail, the sympathetic solicitor from his own pocket makes generous contribution to the sufferer. But the turning of the contents of the hat into the man's lap works a transformation; he is now gayest of the gay, celebrating his good fortune with potations from some bottle drawn from unseen hiding-place, singing senseless songs, and so overwhelming with gratitude the mortified victim of his cunning arts, that our friend would have surely killed the fellow if he only dared.

On the Northern Pacific a juvenile tramp comes on the train. The conductor warns him to leave at the next station, threatening all sorts of mutilation if he should be found on board after the nearest depot is passed. No sooner does the official leave the car, however, than the stalwart brakeman takes the boy, and in the most miscellaneous fashion possible throws him into the huge wood-box in the corner. There all day the fellow rides, lifting the cover from time to time and looking at the passengers without one hint of humor on his dirty face, although we confidently believed that never did the little vagrant feast so royally as on that eventful day.

On the Pacific steamer we are just an hour too late to secure a state-room, and so are placed in a kind of pantry on the second floor down, just above the screw. As we entered our sarcophagus, just before the hour of sailing, we found in the upper berth the shaggiest-looking specimen we had ever seen. His head was bald upon the top, but grown over in the rear with utmost profusion of hair. Snarled and tangled curls and ringlets, — matted, braided, mixed together in such hairy jungle as we had never seen upon a human head! Where the hair left off the beard commenced, — a kind of terra-cotta shade, much faded by the sun. He was a kind of polychromatic man; for his clothes were sea-green, with an outside ulster in a poor combination of black and tan.

We supposed, as we saw him lying there upon the upper shelf, that he was some old mummy, in transit to a San Francisco museum; for he looked for all the world like one of those not over-handsome relics of the past.

When in the early morning he began to unwind himself, preliminary to getting down and out, we had an apprehension that the last day had come, and that sea and land were giving up their dead; for we were feeling a little sea-sick, and did n't care whether the universe wound up or not. As, from beneath our blankets, we saw our room-mate make his hasty toilet, the thought passed through our mind that when this mummy was alive he was, unless his looks deceived, a first-class bandit; and when he asked us for our comb, we presented it as we should all the assets that we had, if only his demand had specified those things. We tried to ask forgiveness for such sins as we could remember, with the headache that we had, and wondered by what process he would kill us when he should have pulled out the few remaining teeth of our relic of a comb. However, one cannot always tell by appearances what men are, in the Great West. The framework of our comb came back to us. The steward was even sought by him and sent to us; and before the voyage was over we found this man the most companionable of fellows, — genial, witty, wise; a graduate of the Edinburgh College of Surgeons, and now a physician practising in some region, to us unknown, between Puget Sound and the North Pole.

The cowboys are often with us, — a trifle loud in manner, with a little flavor of brag and bluster, armed like travelling arsenals, but withal harmless, — not even terrifying, except to the women who have come from the Atlantic coast.

The peanut fiend, like the drum-beat of England, goes round the world. We had hoped that we should get beyond the bounds of his jurisdiction; but he is ubiquitous, — the same irrepressible, inopportune, voluble specimen of importunity in the Territories as in the old centres. In Arizona we found him selling, as native products of the soil, the same shell porte-monnaies that had been tendered us in every State along the way. Corn as hard as Montana agates was offered us as "fresh popped." Novels in green and gold, of the Mrs. Southworth order, were shed upon just and unjust alike; and "Peck's Bad Boy" followed us from sea to sea.

We think it must have been through observation of the newsboys on the trip across the continent that Joseph Cook discovered his theory of the "persistence of evil;" for these pests are simply incorrigible, and if one in desperation throws them from the train, at the next station there will be a new relay come to take up the vacant basket and carry on the work of worrying the martyrs.

There are all sorts of travellers, — good natured, ill natured, inquisitive, and reticent; people who make the best of everything, and those who take the most of everything. An old Scotchwoman rode beside us through three hundred miles of the finest scenery on the continent, and never raised her eyes from the knitting-needles that she held. She had travelled through Europe and Australia in the same fashion, and though she had seen but little, she had filled her trunk half full of the stockings she had made.

Every tourist across the continent is certain to contract the time-table fever somewhere on the trip. It is a species of mania, and usually lasts about three or four days, though we saw several cases where it had become chronic. It usually commences in a study of the guide-book, and is attended in its milder forms with getting off at the various stations, questionings of brakemen and conductors, with interviews with local travellers, which become more persistent as the fever increases in intensity. Then the "map-stage" of the disease comes on; distance tables are studied, and folders of connecting roads, the patient trying to harmonize the figures on the time-table with the actual running time. There is a kind of fascination in the task that lures one on. Plans are made for days and weeks ahead, and once the mania comes on, there is no effectual resistance until the victim is exhausted, or the tables thrown away by solicitous friends. We saw a lamentable case of the disease in New Mexico. At Santa Fé an unsuspicious man came on the train; a departing passenger carelessly left a time-table upon the seat, and the gentleman, all unconscious of the peril of the act, took it up and began to study out its ingenious puzzles. Gradually the subtle fascinations of the folder began to weave themselves over him; the noon-day meal was hastily swallowed that he might resume his work; day deepened into night, and still he puzzled, ciphered, and tried to solve the riddle of the modern Sphinx. We sank to sleep; the poor time-table victim, studying still, was the last object on which our vision rested; and when roused at midnight, at a junction of the roads, by the exodus of a portion of the passengers, we saw on an omnibus top the pitiable sight of the poor victim still studying, in such light as the moon could give, the unsolved and unsolvable riddle.

We had never but once before this trip rode through a night without taking a sleeping car. Coming across the Arizona desert, however, we venture the experiment. It is not a success. Such turnings and twistings, such repeated attempts to make a five-foot-eight man straighten out on a five-foot seat, such complete ignominious failures, we had never experienced before in all the misadventures of a checkered life. We never had much talent in figures. If we were summoned in college, at times, before the faculty, it was not to receive the annual prizes in mathematics; but we learn on that moonlight night upon the desert more of the disciplinary science than we had ever dreamed of in our undergraduate days. We learned that man is not, geometrically considered, a right-angled, triangled kind of a figure; that he cannot successfully be the base and perpendicular of a triangle at the same time; though we gave, in the contortions of our body, a most perfect object-lesson of the spiral of Archimedes. We took up the cushions and half rebuilt the car; we constructed "L's," wings, and additions, with carpet bags and blankets; we tried high pillow made of overcoat and low pillow made of duster; but we worked out the problem to a demonstration, that a full-sized man cannot sleep in the seat of a railway car without building either the car or the man on a different model.

We are persuaded by the experiences of the summer's trip that the most pestilent nuisance to-day in the world of travellers is the man who snores. Pleasant men, men apparently kind-hearted, Christians by day, with the coming on of darkness are transformed into fiends. We had heard snorers in the East without great discomfort, although we have some peculiar theories of what we would do with the mildest of them, if only we had autocratic power. But there is a malignancy in the snoring of these Western fellows that "murders sleep;" it is a kind of interjectional snoring, that rasps the nerves and makes one wild. For a time there is a sort of guttural cadence; the sound grows fainter and fainter, and you think that the end is near; then the music stops, a faint gasp follows, and the hope that springs eternal in the human breast says, "Thank heaven, he is dead at last!" But no, with a series of convulsions, sobs, gasps, and groans, the monster comes back to life, to play over, with endless variations, the same tragedy, until the heart is sick with hope of death deferred. We kicked the elbow of a man half across the State of Missouri, quite as much out of kindness to fellow-passengers as for personal revenge; but it only served to change the snorer's tune, to pull out extra stops in this human organ, and bring down upon ourselves fresh varieties of inharmonious sound. It is said there is no way to cure these fellows except by death. We have spent many wakeful hours during our summer's trip in speculations as to whether, if one should kill a snorer, it would be accounted murder. We would be willing to risk the verdict, if only we could have a hand in making up the jury.

We saw the neatest punishment administered to an obtrusive drummer that ever before came beneath our notice. A pair of young and prepossessing ladies came upon the cars at midnight at a station in New Mexico. We were to change in the early morning, and were riding in the ordinary car. The drummer sat behind the fair young ladies, and was more than kind in his attentions. They did not seem to like it, but hardly knew how to be free from him. One of the ladies was a mother, and had in her arms her infant child.

The young man had evidently been somewhat about the world, and knew that the easiest way into the mother's heart was through the baby; and so he played and toyed with it, snapped his fingers, wound and unwound his stem-winder, and engaged in the various devices that gain the sympathies of a confiding infant. In a moment of forgetfulness he asked to take the child, when the mother passed it over; and the great fellow, in such awkward fashion as men have, dandled and fondled it. It was very pretty and very nice for a time; but a very little of a baby goes a long way with an ordinary man, and it was evident that after a few moments the infant began to be a drug upon the drummer's hands.

Meantime, the mother and her sister, in the seat beyond, have fallen fast asleep, and the obtrusive young man is left alone with a lively baby on his hands to care for as he can. It was a lonesome and a long night for the drummer, for the passengers were profuse in sympathy; and whenever the baby showed signs of sleep, some officious neighbor would slip over and wind the child up for another half-hour of wakefulness. At length the situation became so severe that the drummer gathered boxes and bundles, and, miles away from his destined stopping-place, left the train, throwing the baby in the mother's lap. The woman woke, took the child, but as she looked at the drummer's seat, we judged by the twinkle in her eye that this was not her first journey away from home, and that she carried the baby, perhaps, as a weapon with which to guard the fair sister who sat beside her.

There are touching incidents, too, along the way. More than once mourners come on board and ride beside us, while the precious dead are carried, to the burial-place, in the car beyond. The conductor who was on the train last night going up the branch is with us now as we come back; but another performs his duty, for he is eastward-bound to see once more, if possible, the dying father to whose bedside he was summoned in the night.

For half a day we ride beside an anxious wife, hastening to join her husband, who was shot yesterday in a quarrel up the line; and in the speech with which sorrow finds relief we see, in the long journey of the summer, that no spot upon the earth gives immunity from human suffering.

Now that we are getting homeward, we may give some practical hints about a trip across the continent.

Save for the associations of Europe, — which mean much to cultivated people, and little to others, — a trip to San Francisco and return gives as great enjoyment as a tour to the Old World. In natural scenery, Europe has nothing to be compared to the Yellowstone Park and the Yosemite. Southern California is fairer than Italy in climate, and its peer in vegetation; Mexico can be visited with slight expense of time and money, and Colorado is a museum of wonders. As regards expense, one can make the round trip across the continent at about the expense of a visit to Rome. For seven or eight hundred dollars one can go with great comfort; and a less amount will suffice if one will exercise reasonable prudence. The hotels might be worse; the roads are admirably equipped and well managed. We consider the ideal route is the one which we have described in this book, — out by the way of the Northern Pacific, returning by the Southern Pacific. From Colorado one needs to go west through the Grand Cañon of the Arkansas and over the Marshall Pass; and a slight continuance of the journey takes one to the pretentious humbug of Salt Lake City, which is about all there is on the Central line to the Pacific. During the past summer the long stage-ride over the Rocky Mountains, and the non-completion of the railroad to the Yellowstone Park, would have made this trip difficult for any except those of robust strength; but now the roads are completed, and by another summer all conveniences of travel will be established.

The weather is perfect in the summer months, and during our entire journey neither gossamer nor umbrella were used. Ordinary clothing will suffice; and a small hand-satchel will contain all necessary conveniences.

Expense of travel is somewhat higher than in the East; but with increase of patronage and competition this will be greatly lessened. Travelling is as safe as in any part of the country for one who has ordinary common sense, and is the fortunate owner of a civil tongue; while inevitable discomforts may be reduced to the minimum by a wise disposition to make the best of everything and have a good time.

Eastward now, we are on the home stretch. Chicago is behind us, and through the fair Canadian fields we will hasten as fast as wheels can carry us. Now we halt beside the fair St. Lawrence, where the Thousand Islands float upon the currents of this, the queenliest river that flows in either continent to the sea. Danube, Rhine, and Hudson deserve the praises sung of them; but none of these so worthily might receive the tribute of the poet's song as this grand stream bearing onward its mighty burden.

Not yet has the poet's pen told the wondrous grace of these fair islands here, the little lake set in an island's heart, the balmy days when summer's heat is tempered by the flowing stream, the matchless nights, when the moon works its transformation scenes.

The way homeward now is short; the grain ripens in the Mohawk's valley, and along the Hudson's bank the foliage catches the color of the autumn days. From the metropolis of the Pacific we have come to the larger city on the Atlantic's waters, and our summer's flight from the Brooklyn Bridge to the Golden Gate and back is over, and we are home again.

www.ingramcontent.com/pod-product-compliance
Lightning Source LLC
Chambersburg PA
CBHW031742230426
43669CB00007B/443